D0092572

# FAILURE
# TO
# COMMUNICATE

# FAILURE
# TO
# COMMUNICATE

HOW CONVERSATIONS
GO WRONG AND
WHAT YOU CAN DO
TO RIGHT THEM

## Holly Weeks

HARVARD BUSINESS PRESS
*Boston, Massachusetts*

Copyright 2010 Holly Weeks
All rights reserved
Printed in the United States of America
12  11  10  09  08      5  4  3  2  1

No part of this publication may be reproduced, stored in or introduced into a retrieval system, or transmitted, in any form, or by any means (electronic, mechanical, photocopying, recording, or otherwise), without the prior permission of the publisher. Requests for permission should be directed to permissions@hbsp.harvard.edu, or mailed to Permissions, Harvard Business School Publishing, 60 Harvard Way, Boston, Massachusetts 02163.

Paperback ISBN: 978-1-4221-3749-9

Library of Congress Cataloging-in-Publication Data

Weeks, Holly.
  Failure to communicate : how conversations go wrong and what you can do to right them / Holly Weeks.
     p. cm.
  ISBN-13: 978-1-57851-899-9
  1. Business communication. 2. Interpersonal communication. 3. Oral communication.
I. Title.
  HF5718.W4175 2008
  650.1'3—dc22

                          2008007864

The paper used in this publication meets the requirements of the American National Standard for Permanence of Paper for Publications and Documents in Libraries and Archives Z39.48-1992.

# CONTENTS

## CHAPTER 1

# Introduction

## *When Conversations Go Wrong*

J ACK GRIFFIN and Mike Antonelli became friends in college, where they played hockey at Clarkson.[1] The two small-town Mid-westerners roomed together for their last three years and had stayed in touch when Mike went off to law school in Nebraska and Jack went back to Cleveland and into his family's concrete products business.

While Jack rose through the ranks of the family company, Mike dabbled first in government contracts and then in corporate transactions, never really finding his place. He began to wonder if law school had been a mistake.

By the time Jack was thirty-seven, he had married, renovated an old Victorian in Cleveland Heights, and had three sons. At the same age, Mike was in Seattle, divorced, and restless. The two of them had kept in touch, first meeting up for Grateful Dead concerts and later for golf tournaments. Jack had been a rock while Mike was going through his divorce.

Then Jack's father died of cancer, and Jack became CEO at forty-two. Knowing that Mike was eager for change, Jack called his old friend, inviting him to join the business. Mike had often heard out Jack's idea of expanding the business in the United States and even into China, as well as his fears that the company had languished during his father's final years. Mike had the smarts, the drive, and the people skills to step up the company's metabolism, Jack thought. Mike happily came aboard as senior vice president.

The Cleveland-based company of 270 employees still had a small-company feel. People in different divisions—manufacturing; sales, research, and marketing; and finance and accounting—often knew one another. They were proud of the company's products: large, precast parts ranging from culverts to bridge elements to entire warehouses. The company had even supplied a curved roof for an airport. Jack himself had worked closely with the architect and engineer on that project, and he kept a miniature model of the roof on his desk. It was that project, really, that had given him a taste for new directions. He thought the company could go much further, maybe expanding in the direction of custom mixes and improving the energy-inefficient production of concrete to make it greener. Jack had a vision of taking the established part of the business international and working his way into higher-end products and processes in the United States.

Right from the start, Mike became both Jack's sounding board and his interface with recalcitrant managers. Mike was proud of the vigor of their new vision, and he thought of himself as a persuasive change agent. He put Jack's words about a stepped-up company metabolism into action, quickly tightening some operations and removing underperformers. But the managers were pushing back, and Mike wasn't sure how to react.

For example, in March, Jack had asked Mike to outsource much of the sales function to a subcontractor with more international experience. And Jack wanted it done by September. But at a presentation Mike made to the sales managers in May, they told him that sales wasn't confined to their department alone. Rather, it was integrated into every aspect of the company, including a father-son team in sales and marketing, and a father-daughter pair in sales and research. Mike had expected a few questions about relations with the new firm, and he needed to catch a plane to New York. So he cut into what seemed to be a long-winded story about families with a glance at his watch and a request for any relevant questions. He encouraged people to e-mail him if they had company information to give him. Someone protested that the sales managers were trying to give him a perspective his slides didn't touch on. That didn't sound like a relevant question, so Mike cut that off, too, thanked them, and left. Mike knew this hadn't been his most democratic moment, but Jack's timetable meant he had to move rapidly.

Oddly, Jack's support also seemed to wobble. Jack sometimes criticized Mike's actions as heavy-handed, or made jokes about how slow Mike was to figure out the very company culture he was supposed to change. Once, Jack lost his temper and accused Mike of stepping on his own CEO toes. But an hour later, he caught up with Mike on the way to the dining room, threw his arm across his old friend's shoulders, and joined him for roast-beef sandwiches.

Things came to a head unexpectedly in June, in a senior managers' meeting with Jack. Mike had just been talking about a shift in the organization chart—a shift that would pull research out of its cluster with sales and marketing and make it a more prominent, stand-alone division. If the company intended to push for the greening of the concrete production business, there was a lot of new work to be done, Mike concluded. When he sat back to take questions, the room went quiet. Then Gus, who at fifty-six had been with the company for nearly thirty years and was the most seasoned manager in the room, stood up and pushed a piece of paper toward Jack.

"That's my resignation, Jack, if you want it," Gus said. "Someone has to speak up here, and I guess it will be me."

For the next forty-five minutes, Gus and a few other unhappy veterans turned on Mike. They told Jack that Mike didn't fit with the company, that his simplistic solutions failed to take into account the problems they faced. Gus said that people were afraid to voice their concerns to the man with the hatchet. Managers felt bullied by Mike, not led by Jack. They felt disparaged, and marginalized in their own work. Beyond the managers, there was collateral damage to employees, who were exhausted and mutinous.

Mike turned, ashen-faced, to Jack for support. But Jack was watching Gus.

"I've seen a lot, Jack," Gus said. "Whether I stay or leave, you might want to rethink this new leadership style"—Gus paused and gave Mike a long look—"before any more damage is done."

When Jack finally spoke, it wasn't to Gus. He turned to Mike. "Are you sure," he asked in front of them all, "that you're getting as much professional satisfaction here as you'd like?"

A badly shaken Mike was waiting for Jack at the end of the day. "I've been blocking for you," Mike said. "I've been doing your smackdowns, and the first time I need help, you humiliate me in front of everyone. You've used me, Griff, and betrayed me."

Mike picked up the model of the curved airport roof from Jack's desk and turned it over and over in his hockey-scarred hands, as though to calm himself. In a lower voice, he said, "I left a lot to come here. I can't just walk away from this."

"I brought you here to help you out, Mike," Jack replied. "I wanted to give you a piece of the bigger action. But I had no idea a smart guy like you could know so little about people and make so many mistakes. I'm shoveling up after you every time you talk to someone. But you swagger around as though this was all yours.

You challenge even me. Don't push me too far. What I give I can take away."

## Anatomy of a confrontation: Defining hard talks

Jack and Mike found themselves blindsided in a toxic conversation. It contained elements we all might find familiar. These conversations look and feel like bruising battles, with the power to do real damage. For Mike, the potential damage was easy to see: his job and his oldest friendship were on the line. For Jack, a new senior manager was jeopardizing everything his father and grandfather built. And even closer to home, Jack found himself under attack twice—first challenged publicly by Gus and then challenged privately by Mike. Still worse, whichever way he turned, Jack stood to lose: it looked like either Mike would be out of the company, or Gus would.

At the same time, beyond the verbal warfare, the conversation was emotionally loaded for both men. On one side, Mike had been publicly humiliated; he felt betrayed by Jack. On the other side, Jack was at risk of losing face himself in a very public way, even though he was head of the company. Later in Jack's office, the battle escalated when Mike lashed out at Jack. By that time, Jack was so uncomfortable that he retaliated with real force and heavy threats.

At a third, deeper level, the conversation—a consequence of many other conversations—was complicated by unspoken, even subconscious, intentions and perceptions. Both men were stumbling, blinded by confusion, doubt, and the shock of the unexpected. Jack, on his side, had been frustrated by the contrast between his clear dream and its foggy implementation, but he had been reluctant to criticize his friend Mike outright. So sometimes, Jack said nothing, sometimes he veiled his criticism in humor, and sometimes he vented his frustration in out-and-out anger. Mike, on his side, couldn't read what lay behind Jack's remarks. He knew his own intentions were good, but because legal practice had given him no real management experience, he couldn't change his ineffective, seat-of-the-pants approach to working with the managers. Both Jack and Mike were shocked by how much animosity had built up in the staff before bursting into flame. At that point, Mike had no idea how to recover his balance and save his job. Jack couldn't see how to save his company without sacrificing his oldest friend.

Like Jack and Mike, we all run up against difficult conversations in our professional lives—it's inevitable. (Actually, it's inevitable in our personal lives, too, but this book focuses on work relationships. You can, of course, take home what you learn here.)

Difficult conversations are not inherently bad, any more than a difficult chemistry experiment or a difficult piece of music is inherently bad. But we do struggle with them. While difficult conversations don't often fit neatly into single categories, there are six basic types that give us the most trouble. You can see Jack and Mike, and Gus too, in the mix here.

- **I HAVE BAD NEWS FOR YOU.** A person has to deliver unwelcome information and tries to choose between directness and diplomacy, worried about overplaying on the one hand and understating on the other.

- **YOU'RE CHALLENGING MY POWER.** Someone worries about raising a tough issue with a boss, realizing that there could be significant fallout if the boss thinks it makes him look bad or thinks he's being put on the spot.

- **I CAN'T GO THERE.** Conflict-averse people, even powerful executives, try to avoid difficult conversations altogether, even as they watch a situation—and a relationship—degenerate.

- **YOU WIN/I LOSE.**  No matter how cooperative one person tries to be, her counterpart always tries to come out on top—at her expense.

- **WHAT'S GOING ON HERE?**  A conversation unexpectedly becomes intensely charged and extremely confusing. One side, or both, is assailed for something he didn't say and never intended.

- **I'M BEING ATTACKED!**  A counterpart goes on the offensive with accusations, profanity, shouting, threats, or other aggressive moves.

While any of these can be tough, sometimes, through a combination of forces few of us feel we can control, difficult conversations morph into something more dangerous: they become toxic conversations. Toxic conversations are serious snarls of offense and defense, excruciating emotion, and awful uncertainty. We feel personally damaged by them, and our relationships with our counterparts are damaged by them, too. Sometimes, the damage spreads to a team or other colleagues, to our reputation with clients, or to the company itself.

At the prospect of that kind of fallout, it's understandable that we often try to avoid these conversations at all costs. But when we do, problems just fester, and then, when the tough conversation is finally unavoidable, our situation is worse.

## Transforming hard talks

Even when the power relationship between counterparts is unequal, even when both sides' worst emotions are in play, and even when each side is working with misconceptions about the other, these volatile conversations can be brought into balance. No matter what the power dynamics are or how difficult the subject is, we can reset the course of toxic conversations, unilaterally. By *unilaterally*, I mean on your own, without reacting to your counterpart, and accepting that you can't control what he or she does or thinks.

This book offers a system of strategies and tactics to help us navigate the treacherous minefields we may suddenly find ourselves in when we approach and try to get through—rather than avoid—prickly conversations. Strategies are the thinking part of these conversations, designed here for the realities we face in them. Balanced strategies replace the blanking out, gut reactions, and other horrors that slip in when conversations turn tough and ordinary thinking fails. Tactics are the handling part—what we do in the moment when our counterparts, or our own emotions, are giving us trouble. The system of strategies and tactics in *Failure to Communicate* builds on what I've learned over more than two decades as a communications professional. It works with patterns of trouble I've seen over and over again.

First, the book demonstrates how tough conversations veer into damaging territory when taken on by unprepared and often unskilled parties:

We go in blind → We emerge blindsided

Then, by separating out and shedding light on the many pitfalls we encounter, *Failure to Communicate* shows how a changed mind-set and a set of concrete skills can guide us to resolutions that are more successful:

We go in with skillful tactics → We emerge intact

In the process, we will learn how to avoid treating difficult conversations like warfare, even when our counterpart comes in with a combat mentality. We will learn how to find and keep our balance rather than succumb to our emotions, no matter how our counterpart acts or reacts. We will learn how to avoid mishandling a difficult conversation, even when we can't read our counterpart and don't know how he or she is reading us. And we will learn a set of skills to guide us through the landscape of difficult conversations so that we minimize damage to both sides without giving up or giving in, and without compromising our integrity.

## The landscape of hard talks

It helps to think of a tough conversation as a landscape through which we and our counterpart move. If we look at a landscape expecting to see a battlefield, that's how we will see it. But the landscapes of difficult conversations don't have to be battlefields (although even when they are not, difficult conversations are harder than other conversations). Even when the landscape is *not* a battlefield, however, we can run into all kinds of barriers: swamps to bog us down, unseen pitfalls to trap us, and dead ends.

Meanwhile, if our counterparts have a combat mentality, they are thinking battlefield, and they will put barriers in our way: minefields to block us, stonewalls of silence, or ambushes. Luckily, however, we're not tied to a rope, being dragged into whatever lies in front of us.

In this book, we'll learn how to take a longer view—a satellite perspective—on these conversations, while we're in them. With that, we will have a clearer sense of the landscape, and we can see where conversations are likely to snarl and what's preventing us from reaching our goals.

I like to think of the conversational landscape as if it were a *parkour* landscape that we're going to make our way through. If you've seen the opening chase scene in *Casino Royale*, the 2006 James Bond movie, you've seen parkour in action, albeit with considerable dramatic license. James Bond and his quarry—both called *traceurs* in parkour—move through a tough landscape, full of surprises, using leaps, vaults, rolls, and landings to surmount obstacles in their path. David Belle, who created parkour, might wince at the competitive force of the movie chase, because he believes parkour is a philosophical way of moving through the world, not a competitive sport. But he would recognize the skill and balance the two used to handle the landscape in which Bond and his target found themselves, and Belle knows that unpredictable things can happen.

In our own hard conversations, if we combine a satellite view and a parkour approach, we can begin to see where we are, where we could move, where our counterparts are, and where they are likely to move. We can begin to see the conversational landscape unfolding in a more recognizable and manageable way.

And we will be able to work the landscape, like parkour traceurs, instead of battling through it.

## The origins of *Failure to Communicate*

This book grew out of earlier books on difficult conversations, but its goal is different and its methods tackle a whole new set of circumstances. Many earlier books, such as *Taking Charge of Organizational Conflict: A Guide to Managing Anger and Confrontation*, and *Resolving Conflicts at Work: Eight Strategies for Everyone on the Job*, look at how to *prevent* difficult conversations. A preventive book might address a discrimination charge brought by one colleague against another by showing managers how to identify problems in the early stages and next time nip conflict in the bud, so that no similar problem happens again.

A second type of book looks at well-meaning people who are at odds because of a misunderstanding. Those books, such as *Difficult Conversations: How to Discuss What Matters Most*, focus on clearing up a misunderstanding, ending the trouble that the misunderstanding caused, and returning people to their good relationship. I refer to these conversations as "soft" difficult conversations, because goodwill goes a long way in helping people through them.

This book will help you prevent certain conversations that don't belong in the workplace, and it will help you clear up misunderstandings. But its true purpose is to help you handle conversations of an altogether greater magnitude of difficulty. When people carry a combat mentality, as well as painful emotions, into a conversation with unseen problems, goodwill is not enough to prevent damage on both sides.

My method has emerged from twenty-five years of teaching at the Harvard Business School, Harvard's Graduate School of Education and Kennedy School of Government, Radcliffe Seminars Management Program, and Simmons School of Management, and from working as a coach and consultant with a wonderfully diverse roster of clients—from investment firms and hospitals to tech start-ups and sports agencies. With students and clients alike, I found that although each tough conversation between a pair of counterparts was unique, taken together the conversations began to fall apart in recognizable patterns. Even good communicators fouled up in conversations when one or both sides fell into the combat mentality, when their emotional buttons were pushed, and when there was a breakdown between what one side intended and the other side heard. In almost every case, people who were floundering in difficult conversations were well intentioned; they didn't lack the will to do well, but they couldn't think usefully about what was happening or about how to get good results. And even when smart people could see where their problems lay, it was very hard for them to change what they did—they simply didn't have other strategies and tactics to try.

And there was nothing simple about the situations in which they found themselves. People had been struggling in conversations that made them bleed, with counterparts who had their own concerns—not theirs—in mind at the time. *Both* sides needed a book to help them handle not the "soft" talks, but those "hard," often toxic, conversations.

*Failure to Communicate* addresses fundamental questions raised by very hard conversations:

- How do you talk about a difficult issue with someone who refuses to reason? Someone who lies? Someone who threatens you? Someone who has more power than you have and is ready to use it?

- If someone starts bullying you, how do you know whether to retaliate or take the punch?

- What if the person catches you off guard? How do you keep from getting backed into a corner?

- What if you're so anxious that you blank out, or you're so angry that you lose control? If you say something you wish you could take back, can you do it without looking weak?

- What if you're in the wrong? How can you avoid losing face?

- What if the other person knows what she's doing and you don't?

## Bringing balance and skill to bear

A lot of tough variables complicate our difficult conversations. Some variables apply to us and some don't—but even those that don't affect us can apply to our counterparts and undermine our conversations with them. But whatever variables are in play, the common thread in these conversations is that they are so badly off-kilter. One way or another, the people in them are thrown off balance again and again. We are swept up in strong emotions, or we are blundering through misperceptions and uncertainty, or the conversations themselves are constantly sliding into warfare. This book provides us with better skills to bring difficult conversations into better balance.

*Failure to Communicate* takes a canny look at the strategies and tactics that real people need in real difficult conversations. It does not assume that with a small change or two, the complex landscape of a difficult conversation will smooth out into open savanna with a well-marked road to success running through it. *Failure to Communicate* builds an approach that is flexible enough to steer you through all kinds of tough conversations and broad enough that you don't need to learn a different set of skills for every variable you meet.

This book doesn't assume that everyone is on the same side in a difficult conversation and it doesn't overlook power plays, but it does give us the skills we need to deal with the imbalances we face. It acknowledges that strong emotion is a real factor in these conversations, but that we can have emotions without bowing to them. Finally, this book gives us strategies for moving forward, even when we're on uncertain terrain, so that we don't have to guess how to handle difficult counterparts or complicated situations.

You will come away with a sense of navigating through difficult conversations in a way that is more like parkour's combination of sport and philosophy than it is like war. Parkour is a way to train the body and mind to react to obstacles in the landscape appropriately, with techniques that work. Like parkour, the approach in *Failure to Communicate* is not competitive—there's no point in trying to "win." It's not a series of gimmicks or tricks. As in parkour, the intention is to make your way with balance and skill through the landscape in which you find yourself. Difficult conversations have an added challenge: they come with a counterpart who shares the landscape, someone who may be side by side with you one minute and pushing against you the next.

The skills you learn in *Failure to Communicate*—and the balance you find and maintain—are ultimately about more than navigating the landscape of any one conversation. They are skills that will make you a better colleague, a better leader, and a better human being. They are not sometime skills that you turn on and off, depending on your conversation or your counterpart. Perhaps most important, becoming skillful means not just knowing where you want to go in a conversation or how you want to get there, but knowing who you want to be.

## Remember:

- The warfare, troubling emotions, and sheer uncertainty of difficult conversations can do real damage to people and their relationships.

- Tough conversations fall apart in recognizable ways.

- Good strategies and tactics can bring tough conversations into balance.

- We can change the direction and outcome of tough conversations unilaterally.

## CHAPTER 2

# Anatomy of Hard Talks

SUPREME COURT JUSTICE Potter Stewart said he was certain he could tell when he was looking at hard-core pornography because "I know it when I see it."[1] In our case, we recognize hard talks because we know them when we're in them. Sometimes, that's as far as we get in putting our finger on what's really going wrong. But we can, and should, take a closer look to see what makes a conversation fail.

Let's look at a showdown between two software product managers, Carl and Ernesto. A conversation between them failed at several points for several reasons. If we were to read through the conversation and then go back and try to prevent their confrontation from happening in the first place, we could point to obvious problems and ways to avoid them. But in a live conversation, the characteristics that make the conversation fail, and what to do about them, are not obvious.

As two product managers working together on a software-company team, Carl and Ernesto were in conflict over how much time should be devoted to a single project: enhancing the supply-chain software. Ernesto was deeply involved in the project and had put a lot of time and energy into it, sometimes at the expense of other work. Carl and others on the team had been picking up the slack, but the feeling that Ernesto got special treatment was building.

Finally, Carl took up the problem with Abby, the CEO, on a trip to the home office. "I admire Ernesto's dedication to the supply-chain software. I wish I could bottle it," Carl told Abby. "But we're a team, and Ernesto is working more like an individual contributor. Not only are other projects starting to slip, but our cohesiveness as a team is also eroding. I hate to do it, but I seriously think I have to take him off that project." Abby listened, sighed with regret, and agreed that Carl was right.

But Ernesto was stunned when Carl told him that he was off the project and that Abby had agreed to the decision. He couldn't just take Carl's blow on the chin. "You went behind my back," Ernesto said, furious. "You know how important this project is. I can't do everything at once, even when I want to. Is controlling me the only thing that's important to you?"

Carl was startled by the "control" slant Ernesto had taken, but he tried to be reasonable. "We've gone over this again and again," Carl said, as calmly as he could. "You always agree that you can, and will, manage your time better. But then you lapse. And while you tunnel down on this project, everyone else has to scramble to cover your other responsibilities. It isn't working, Ernesto. You know that."

But Ernesto ignored the time-management issue and attacked Carl again. "You talk a good line about joint decision making, but when you don't get what you want, suddenly it's top-down control," Ernesto accused him. "And you're not even honest about it."

Carl had known Ernesto would be disappointed, but he was shaken by Ernesto's anger and aggression. How could they work together now?

This conversation between Carl and Ernesto is unique, as every difficult conversation is. But surprisingly, what separates difficult conversations from normal conversations is not as individual as we might think. Across the board, there are three traits—with real costs—that make difficult conversations categorically different.

## Three basic traits of hard talks

First, there is the *combat mentality*, the attitude that difficult conversations are battles with winners and losers. In the showdown with Carl, Ernesto took on a combat mentality as soon as he heard the news that he would no longer be on the supply-chain project. From that combat perspective, he took Carl's decision as an unprovoked attack, and he retaliated with a counterattack of his own. Once the combat mentality took hold of Ernesto, his experience of the whole conversation was colored by how he saw Carl's ploys. He took Carl's first message as a stab in the back.

But a combat mentality is not limited to one side—Carl, on his side, took Ernesto's salvos as character assassination. Such a charged ploy is hard to take and hard to handle. Talking with people who struggle after a conversation has turned into battle, I hear again and again that their whole framework for conversation of any kind was instantly reduced to a question of how to fight, or how to fight back. Carl himself said after his debacle with Ernesto, "I thought we were going to talk, and it turned into a confrontation. I was on the spot, and I didn't know what to do." The bigger problem is not a single maneuver, however tough, but the combat mentality itself: it treats conversation like a battlefield and sets the stage—and the expectations—for war. It is a central reason for the real and lasting damage that these conversations cause between people.

The second trait setting difficult conversations apart is that they carry heavier *emotional loads*—particularly anger, embarrassment, anxiety, or fear—than normal conversations do. Just as we don't know how to handle combat maneuvers, we don't know how to handle a conversation when our own emotions are in the way. During their showdown, Carl was unnerved by the thrusts from Ernesto—claims that Carl was controlling and deceitful—in response to Carl's own explicit efforts to be reasonable and low-key. The accusations made Carl nervous; he didn't know what to do. So he stuck with an approach that plainly wasn't working, since it didn't disarm Ernesto. From Carl's point of view, Ernesto clearly was *not* trying to be reasonable. Instead, it seemed to Carl, Ernesto was working hard to make the conversation worse.

But, of course, heavy emotional loads are a two-way street. On his side, Ernesto was agitated by his own emotional reactions to what he was hearing. From his point of view, Carl was the one not trying at all to have the conversation go well. To make matters worse, one awkward, embarrassing, or annoying conversation rarely puts a stop to a tough problem. There will be others. And because Carl and Ernesto are still on the same product team, both the emotions and the combat mentality set in play between them are bound to raise their heads again.

The third trait of difficult conversations is that it's *hard to read* what's happening. It's hard to read the other side's intentions. And it's hard to tell how our counterpart is taking what we say, and then how he feels in reaction. In Carl and Ernesto's showdown, neither side could read the other well: there was a real breakdown between Carl's intention to tell Ernesto about a decision he had made, aimed at evening out the team's workload, and the way Ernesto read it. Then there was a second breakdown between Ernesto's intention not to take the news lying down and the way Carl read that. Each side formed misconceptions based on his own perspective, unable to read the other's intentions.

There was still one more breakdown—between intentions and perceptions that were not even on Carl or Ernesto's radar. In his own view, Ernesto was knocking himself out to give the supply-chain software the development it deserved while doing his best to hold up his end on other projects, however imperfectly. His intentions were good, and he thought he deserved support and praise. But that's not how Carl read the situation. He saw the resentment building up in the team because of Ernesto's single focus, and he reacted, with good intentions, to that resentment. It never occurred to Carl to praise Ernesto for creating a burden on others. Ernesto's expectation simply wasn't on Carl's radar.

So taken together, what have Carl and Ernesto got now? A militaristic, emotionally loaded, misconception-filled exchange that is hard to read. The truth is that just one major pitfall—the combat mentality, emotional load, or a breakdown over misconceptions—can make a difficult conversation suddenly, or even predictably, go south. But in practice, we rarely deal with just one of them at a time. They tend to hit a difficult conversation all snarled together, the way they did for Carl and Ernesto.

The difference between bearably tough conversations and toxic ones comes down to how hard they hit. A bearable conversation might have an emotional component—it could be tense or uneasy. A bearable conversation might also include confusion or uncertainty—it could involve a misunderstanding or a disagreement. And a bearable conversation might have one counterpart who has more power than the other. A toxic conversation, however, is a lot more than a little uncomfortable, a little confusing, or a little lopsided. Toxic conversations are like Carl and Ernesto's, or Jack and Mike's in chapter 1. We really struggle to get through them. They mutate into combat. They cause pain, and they damage relationships and reputations. The stakes are high for at least one side, and often for both. And tough talks like these don't work out most of the time, not the way regular conversations do.

This is quite a tangle. These talks are not just hard to handle, they are hard to think about.

## Three familiar, but misguided, slants on handling hard talks

For just those reasons, people bring three conventional ideas to tough conversations, ideas that are *not* hard to think about: (1) tough conversations are simple, (2) we can win them, and (3) they aren't our fault. These are familiar and even comforting slants on hard talks, and it makes sense, especially when tension is high, to fall back on what's familiar. But because these long-standing ideas aren't quite right, they are also risky.

## Oversimplification

We have a stake in making difficult conversations simpler. No one wants to try to pull apart that snarl of combat mentality, emotional loads, and misconceptions when we are looking for the cause of our trouble. The easiest way to make it all simpler is to point to one thing that's the real problem. Understandably, a lot of us try to do that, and we usually finger the subject of the conversation or the other person. Getting it down to one culprit makes sense, but it also gives us another problem.

The conversation's *subject* can be trouble. Some subjects are definitely more charged than others: every time you touch them, something bad happens. A plant closing, for example, is sometimes such a charged subject that people just dodge it. In fact, before a plant closes, managers often repeatedly assure people that the plant will stay open. Then, when the plant finally does close, any conversation about it sets off anger and distrust in people who had listened to, and believed, the early reassurances. It appears that the subject of the plant closing is the problem, and managers will sigh, "There's no way to give bad news well."

Likewise, our *counterpart* can be tough. There can be personal strain between the two of us, and we expect to have a hard time talking. In other cases, we're up against a boss who has more power and can hurt us if a tough conversation goes badly. Ironically, it isn't much easier for the boss, because bosses worry about their own managerial competence if a conversation with a difficult counterpart conflicts with how they think they ought to have handled it.

But the trouble here is that seeing just the subject or just the counterpart as the problem leads to oversimplifying what's going wrong. Why is that risky? Because we stop there. We can give up on a subject (like plant closings) or pin the blame for the difficult conversation on our counterpart (like a more powerful boss) and stop. That's a problem simply because there's much more in play during a difficult conversation than what people are talking about and whom they are talking to. Blocking out the rest won't make it easier to get through the conversation itself in good shape. It didn't work for Claire.

Claire, a graphic designer, liked being friends with her clients, and was nonconfrontational by nature. She thought particular subjects, like a disagreement about money, automatically put a conversation out of bounds. "It's very hard, practically impossible, for me to discuss differences over costs with clients," she said. "I don't want them to be dissatisfied with my work, and then with me. So if clients bicker over a bill, I give up, even when the charges are consistent with the original estimate plus the changes they asked for." But Claire gave up so quickly that more than one client got used to asking for a cost adjustment.

There was the case of Tony, a jeweler and store owner whose shop was in the same building as Claire's studio, and who had asked Claire to design marketing materials for him. He was pleased with the outcome, and they agreed that Tony would get a discount in exchange for acknowledging Claire as the designer in the new brochure. Tony then asked Claire to incorporate part of the design on new business cards for him.

"That's a little harder than it looks, Tony," Claire told him. "I'll need to modify the design to fit with the smaller scale of the cards, but it will still coordinate with the materials and it will look great. I'll show you a sample next week."

Again, Tony was happy with the design, but when he got the bill, he called Claire. "Great cards, Claire, but the discount doesn't show on the bill. It's the slow season, which is why I could focus on this stuff, but that's also why I can only do it at a discount. Do you just want to just send me a corrected bill? Oh, and are you coming to the wine and cheese party in my workshop on Thursday?"

Claire explained that the bill was correct. "The discount was for the brochure, Tony, remember? Because you gave me that nice acknowledgment? This design for the cards had to be done differently, remember? It's a different job."

"Yes, sure, I remember." Tony said. "I did think of them as pretty much the same, though. The cards are marketing material, too. But, okay, how about if you give me a 'good neighbor' discount to help me out?"

The case that Tony made was too sweet to say no to, so Claire gave in. But six months later, Tony again asked for a discount after she had clearly told him the cost of a job.

"This isn't fair, Tony." Claire told him, her voice shaky. "You always put me in such an awkward position. I give you the lowest price I can, lower than I should. But it's never low enough. You shouldn't ask me to do it for less."

Tony was completely thrown. "I had no idea that this was how you felt," he said. "This is the first I've heard that you thought I was trying to take advantage of you, maybe even trying to cheat you. No one's ever said that about me before. I'm sorry I asked."

Then Tony said, quite formally, "I will pay your bill in full, of course. I'm sorry I ever asked for any of this."


What happened between Claire and Tony was a pattern. Over and over again, Claire got stuck in conversations that damaged her business and her friendships with clients. Unintentionally, by giving in on costs to sidestep a disagreement over them, Claire encouraged clients to bring up the very subject—money—that she dreaded. Then she blamed her clients for forcing the difficult conversations she wanted to avoid. Her reaction startled and confused clients like Tony, whose own reaction then started new conflicts and new difficult conversations. The relationships that had been important to Claire in the first place deteriorated, or ended.

But when conversation after conversation failed, the lesson Claire took away—that the subject of money was toxic—made her real problem worse. With her narrow focus, considering only the subject and vowing to avoid it, she couldn't stand back and see the landscape of conversations as they unfolded. She couldn't see herself slide into the combat mentality. She couldn't see the misperceptions on both sides, and she couldn't see that her reactions to both of those were raising the emotional stakes for her. Claire's tunnel vision trapped her in the same pattern time and again, even when the approach she used was clearly not working.

It's understandable that people want to reduce the number of factors they have to handle to get through difficult conversations. But these conversations are simply too big for that. If we reduce our understanding to just the subject, or just the counterpart, or any other single angle, we won't see other obstacles in the landscape of the conversation we need to move through. That can make us misjudge what's wrong, where a conversation is likely to go off the rails, and how what we're doing is working out. And because difficult conversations *are* genuinely complicated, oversimplifying them can make a tough situation worse.

### The win-or-lose mentality

"Simple is easier" is one long-standing idea about tough conversations that isn't quite right. Another is that conversations are to be "won," like races or card games. But the cost of winning a tough conversation is high: if others think we won at their expense, payback can be both damaging and long-term. But with the notion of winning or losing a conversation in mind, both sides think that if they try to undo damage they've done or try to recover from a mistake, they'll look weak, lose face, or appear to be backing down. Nothing makes a difficult conversation go from bad to worse faster than two counterparts who can see it going wrong, but imagine they'll lose if they back up and try to set it right.

### The delusion of good intentions

There is one more familiar idea that leads us to blame the counterpart when the conversation goes badly. It's what I call "the delusion of good intentions"—the idea that difficult conversations shouldn't go badly for us or even happen to us at all, because we mean well and try to do well. It's never wrong to have good intentions, but it's also not enough. If the counterpart means well, too, whom will *she* blame?

The delusion of good intentions also has a flip side. When a difficult conversation gets stressful or downright harrowing, we rightfully worry about the combat ploys that our counterparts might use. But we go wrong when we think that their ploys are directly driven by their motives. If their ploys are harsh, we think they are willfully harsh. At the same time, our counterparts are likely to think the same about us and are reacting to the way they read our tactics. Nothing escalates difficult conversations more than each side's feeling provoked by the other and justified in his own response.


We're in a horrible position. What's simple and familiar doesn't work well, but the real underbelly of difficult conversation—the combat mentality, the emotional load, and the misperceptions breakdown—is hard to look at, because we don't know what to do with it. Intentions and misperceptions, combat maneuvers and provocations, embarrassment and fear all snarl together into a mess, even when we're trying to make our situation more manageable. Still, this is the tough, threatening, and confusing anatomy at the heart of difficult conversations, and we need to deal with it. We can't get through these conversations if we don't look more closely at what we—and our counterparts—actually *do* that makes difficult conversations go bad.

## Remember:

- The combat mentality makes us treat difficult conversations like battlefields with winners and losers.

- Our own emotions get in our way—particularly anger, embarrassment, and fear.

- Intentions and perceptions on both sides are hard to read.

- Our simple and familiar ideas about how to handle tough conversations don't help us.

## CHAPTER 3

# What's Wrong with What We Do

WHO IS RESPONSIBLE when a difficult conversation starts down the slippery slope to failure? What role does our counterpart play in goosing it along? For that matter, what do *we* do that makes a conversation worse?

There's no question that we think more than 50 percent of the trouble in a difficult conversation is on the other side, particularly when our own intentions are good. Does it matter? If we're following the combat model, not so much. The combat mentality does put a big emphasis on the question of who is in the wrong, because that helps us know whether we deserve to win. Unfortunately, of course, our counterpart is thinking along the very same line we are—that more than 50 percent of the trouble is on *our* side. In the conversation between us, they cancel each other out.

Looking back to Carl and Ernesto in chapter 2, whose fault was the breakdown there? The real answer is that in these conversations, fault is in the eye of the beholder. Ernesto thought Carl started the breakdown when Carl told him he was off the software project that he, Ernesto, was so invested in. (Had he read chapter 1 of this book, Ernesto would have recognized this tough conversation as the type I called "I have bad news for you.") But from Carl's point of view, Ernesto's aggressive reaction to a reasonable approach started the breakdown. (Carl would have seen this conversation as the "I'm being attacked!" type.) And to be realistic, in a failing conversation, neither side is going to accept the other side's opinion of who is at fault. Each side feels provoked by the other and feels justified in his response.

Even though the habit of assigning blame is a familiar one, the question "Whose fault?" sends us down the wrong path. It's a dead-ender in terms of skill—we stop at "your fault" (or, less often, "my bad"), and then it's game over. Fixing blame doesn't help us handle a difficult conversation better; it only exaggerates the differences between us, even when we're sure we're right, pushing an already tough conversation farther out of balance. But if, instead, we look into some of the basic dynamics operating on the two sides—if we can see what's really going on in these conversations—we can change the way we handle them and the way they work out. Let's start with what our counterparts are doing—even if it's not true that their sole purpose is to make our lives miserable.

## What *they* do

The single greatest hope most of us bring to a difficult conversation is that our counterpart won't start trouble and that we can get on with it normally. If that worked out, though, we wouldn't think the conversation was difficult to begin with. We can gather under one umbrella all the ways a counterpart does give us a hard time—they are called *thwarting ploys*. The function of thwarting ploys is to get us to back off, to make our counterparts themselves come out on top, or to get out of the conversation altogether.

There's a whole arsenal of thwarting ploys out there—some defensive, some offensive, and some both. The most successful ones, however, have something in common: it's hard to be sure that we're reading them right.

Take, as an example, a colleague who makes a derogatory re-mark to a teammate in front of the rest of the team and, when the teammate later complains in private, says, "Just kidding. Are you always so touchy?" It's easy to put a passive-aggressive label on that one-two, public-private punch. But the label doesn't help us handle either remark. If the first remark hit home, how should the teammate respond to it in front of the team, where the dam-age was done? For that matter, what does he say in private to the second punch?

Here's a second example, one that's almost universally toxic: a supervisor is giving feedback to a new hire on her handling of a customer's issue. The new hire gets very quiet, her eyes redden, and she starts to cry. To the supervisor, her reaction is inexplica-ble; he can't read it at all. But his emotions are in a knot: he is acutely embarrassed, he is angry that he might be in the hands of a manipulator, and, at the same time, he is worried that there is more going on behind the tears than he can handle.

He also thinks that knowing the intention behind the ploy is the only way he will know how to respond to the ploy itself. Is she trying to manipulate him, or not? Unless he asks her motive—and believes what she says—he simply doesn't know. And his strong reaction is a very bad base from which to make a good assumption.

Although we can't tell the intention behind a thwarting ploy, right or wrong, we often think we know exactly what it is. That complicates the third example, which concerns a manager who reportedly crossed a line with a subordinate into what could be construed as harassment. When his senior manager spoke to him, the manager said, "That never happened. If you repeat it, I'll sue you myself for racial discrimination."

Immediately, his senior manager believed she knew the purpose of the manager's threatening ploy: to stop the conversation right there. However, in a situation as tense and uncertain as this one, there is a real problem with assuming the intentions behind a thwarting ploy: it shuts out the possibility that the manager wasn't using a thwarting ploy at all, but was staunchly telling the truth and clearly stating his course of action. Thwarting ploy, or not?

We don't know. Every day, we are dealing not only with people who are trying to thwart us, but also with people who are not. And sometimes, people are just testing how we will react. The problem is we can't tell which is which. We need a plan for handling this kind of ambiguity, for the simple reason that uncertainty is a hallmark of difficult conversation. But we haven't got a plan.

## What *we* do

There's no question that thwarting ploys work against us. But we're players in these conversations, too—they don't just *happen* to us. The truth is that we bring a lot of trouble with us to our own conversations. There are five ways we go wrong and, in doing so, make a bad situation worse.

### Avoid confrontation

One manager simply calls these the conversations you don't want to wake up and do. Except for highly aggressive people, everyone's first choice is avoidance. What's wrong with avoidance? About the same thing that's wrong with closing your eyes to other problems—the situation tends to get worse.

Henry, the CEO of a fast-growing specialty foods company that had gained a sudden national reputation, had recently hired Jennifer as communications director. Right away, Jennifer had worked up a groundbreaking speech for Henry to take around the country as he met with executives of major companies who had a real interest in Henry and his business. In place of the talking points Henry was used to, Jennifer had put together a tight script cuing up the slides. She had revamped his usual style, first, because this speech was so important and, second, because she wanted Henry to start putting across a more polished image. At first, Henry balked. He knew his business perfectly well, and he liked talking conversationally—not speechifying—about it. But eventually, Henry reluctantly agreed to the new approach, partly because that's why he had hired a communications director in the first place and partly because he was conflict-averse and didn't want to argue with Jennifer anymore.

But when it got down to the wire, Henry didn't go with the plan. While he was out of town for the very first meeting, he hired a freelance speechwriter at considerable expense to work up an entirely new presentation—not with a script nailed tight to slides, but with the talking points that suited the way his mind worked. He told the speechwriter, "Help me do what I want to do. Don't tell me what I ought to do instead."

By the time Henry got back to the home office, Jennifer—and everyone else—had heard about the speechwriter and the change. The first time Henry saw Jennifer, he said to her, "Thanks for everything you did. I couldn't have done it without you." Jennifer felt undermined, humiliated, and angry.

Above all, Henry wanted to sidestep a confrontation. (For him, the conversation with Jennifer—or rather, the lack of it—fell into the "I can't go there" category.) He did, in fact, have the conversation he needed to have, but he had it with the out-of-town speechwriter, not with Jennifer, his own director of communications. On her side, Jennifer didn't interpret Henry's actions as nonconfrontational; she thought he had set her up and let her fail. (Jennifer saw the same absentee conversation as the type called "You win/I lose.") When Henry thanked Jennifer, she didn't hear an attempt to smooth ruffled feathers; she heard sarcasm. Their working relationship never recovered from this breakdown. Jennifer left the company, taking most of her staff with her—a disruptive and expensive solution to Henry's problem. In the end, of course, both sides lost.

### Find our own emotions in the way

While one manager calls these "the conversations you don't want to wake up and do," another says she knows six-foot-three, seven-figure executives who cannot bring themselves to tell a subordinate who is doing well that, in addition to her strengths, she has a weakness. Why? They don't want to hurt her feelings. That sounds as though the problem is the other person's feelings. That may be part of the problem, but it is our own reluctance, an unhelpful feeling itself, that stalls the conversation before it starts.

Like the tall, kindhearted executives, Henry and Jennifer didn't want to hurt each other's feelings. These were not two people lashing out at each other—this difficult conversation was damaging because the conversation essentially was not happening at all *between* the two of them. Instead, the trouble was isolated *within* each of them. Both people were angry and embarrassed, and because they were, both bypassed a conversation they needed to have to work out the very thing that angered and embarrassed them.

Emotions don't get in our way only when we clamp a lid on them, the way Henry and Jennifer did. Ernesto, the software product manager in chapter 2, tripped up when his emotions burst out and walloped Carl. These three used their emotional reactions as reason to strike at their counterparts. While Ernesto struck at Carl during their conversation, Henry had avoided his own conversation with Jennifer. So his annoyance and frustration didn't burst out, but did leak out when he undermined Jennifer by hiring the speechwriter without telling her. Jennifer's humiliation and anger didn't burst out, either, but she followed Henry's lead by quitting and taking her staff—without telling him. Whether expressed in the conversation or suppressed until later, emotional reactions spawn thwarting tactics of their own.

### Swing from pole to pole

In a confrontation, particularly a surprise "You're attacking me!" type, some people don't know whether to take the punch or retaliate. Their problem is that they can see passivity and they can see aggression, but they can't see middle ground between the two. Unhappy with both extremes, they will use a sequence of the two. "I held back as long as I could, but when that didn't work, I had no choice except to strike out," they will say later.

That's what Vivek, a young tech team member, did. As he led his first team meeting on an advanced protocol, the group was becoming restive. Vivek was slow, nervous, and tentative, and he knew the team was used to a faster pace. Still, he was caught off guard when Mack assaulted him about a task decision. "That would be a dumb move, guy," Mack drawled. "No one here will get behind that."

It was hard for Vivek to know how to respond. He didn't have an easy wit or American self-confidence. He couldn't gauge how casually or intensely the hit was meant. And these were his peers—he wasn't their manager. He knew the others would judge him by his response to Mack.

He let the remark pass, and the next one, too. Mack baited him a third time. "Wrong again, my man," Mack said. "I've seen that bush-league approach before. It doesn't work. Just pull the trigger, and put it out of its misery. What else have you got?"

This time, Vivek broke the pattern. He walked over to Mack's table and leaned across. "Get out," he said. "If you want to get back in, get a manager to back you." At the end of the afternoon, Vivek's own manager took him aside and told him that he was reconsidering whether Vivek should be leading sessions at all if he couldn't control his temper.

Vivek was using what I call the "take it, take it . . . have a cow" technique, and it's not a good one. It gets its start from tension between two poles. On the one hand, we don't want to be negative, and on the other, we don't want to be pushed around. So, like Vivek, we whiplash from nice guy to adversary. Neither seems right, and neither is. The exaggerated swing is hard on relationships and on your reputation. But if Vivek tries to give it up, he might replace it with a single approach to difficult conversations that seems safe and stick with it, right or wrong.

### Stick to one old stand-by

Sticking with an approach that looks safe and workable sounds like a better plan than swinging from one extreme to the other. But it, too, has a downside. Those with very few options for handling a difficult conversation are caught in a bind: they don't have much to work with, so if the first thing they try doesn't work, they do it *more*. In fact, like Henry, the speechmaking CEO, we can be aware of our weakness for years and still not know how to correct or compensate for it.

Gail, a physician with high standards for others, was quick to lay into fellow staff or associates for shortcomings, real or perceived. She would make cutting remarks to them in front of colleagues or patients. Later in private, she would apologize, excusing her quick temper on the grounds that it was the result of her high standards around health care. Gail's apologies were short monologues, however; if a staff member tried to speak of standards of his or her own, she would walk away, saying, "I said I was sorry, didn't I?" This public abuse and private excusing went on year after year, despite the high turnover on Gail's staff. The apologies weren't working. When Gail had to ask other staff in the physician group to fill in for her, she began to apologize in advance for any offense she might cause, but even so, the others often refused to help her out. Eventually, her partners told her they were dropping her specialty, but when Gail left, they picked it up again, with a new practitioner.

This doctor simply sounds like a jerk whose behavior should never be tolerated, certainly not year after year. But there's more to this. Gail grew up in a working-class military family where people dealt with one another at high volume and straight from the shoulder. She believed, as they did, that the best way to address a problem was to nip it in the bud. Her sergeant father had instilled

high standards in all his children, treating them as he did his sol-
diers—with concern for their welfare, but not softly. And he
taught his children to treat everyone the same. Without the pressure of high standards, Gail would never have gotten out of her
neighborhood and into college, never mind medical school. And
she was a superb physician. Matters of life and death were not
clichés to her.

Gail was not reacting to an emotional overload. In fact, she
didn't even think she was in a difficult conversation, until her
remarks met with a poor reception. At the same time, she was not
ill-intentioned. Gail was vigorous about her own mistakes, and she
genuinely didn't think that telling people they were making a mistake was a problem. Nevertheless, Gail *had* learned that she caused
trouble, and while it didn't come naturally to her, she *had* figured
out what to do about it—apologize. But when "sorry" didn't work,
it didn't occur to her to try something else. And the root of that
problem was Gail's inability to see how people were reading her.
The cost to her reputation and relationships was very high.

### Resist skill

Finally, although we want to know what to do in difficult conversations, something in us resists the idea of getting good at
handling them. What holds us back?

Habit alone can make us resist skill. If we think that all difficult
conversations are fights or debates that we never win, and we have a
history of bad experiences, then we probably will hunker down and
resist a new skill because we don't know whether it will work. And
if it doesn't, we'll only make our situation worse. Why chance it?

Some people have an entirely different reason. They resist skill
because they hate being manipulative. They have been in conversations with counterparts who have tried to get the upper hand,
using one ploy or another, and they don't want to do that to other
people. To them, "skillful" and "conniving" appear to be about
the same. Honesty and good intentions, they believe, ought to be
enough to get them through a difficult conversation.

And many people simply find it much easier to have any conversation, and certainly a difficult conversation, with someone who handles it the same way they do. Win or lose, an engineer will be okay arguing with other engineers, because they are likely to use tight, fact-based arguments like his own. It simply feels like the right way to argue. Increasing skill just sounds like getting squishy. They don't want to get anywhere near that.

## It takes two

Taken together, chapters 2 and 3 have shown us that tough conversations are complex, however fervently we want them to be simple. They are complicated not just by the subjects that spawn the conversations themselves, but also by the ploys our counterparts bring to hard talks and by the habits we bring.

In these chapters, we have teased apart the complications, particularly the worst pitfalls of the combat mentality, heavy emotional loads, and the misconceptions breakdown. But in practice, difficult conversations can fill up with all that, plus a snarl of thwarting ploys, doubts, and reactions—each side feeding into and feeding off what happens on the other side. And now we have to multiply everything by two, because what we do in a difficult conversation is as provocative, and hard for our counterparts to read, as what they do is for us. And our skills in handling these conversations are as likely as theirs are to fall short. No wonder our first choice is to avoid tough conversations altogether. However, we need something better to do when we can't get around them.

To get where we want to go, we need to change what we have been doing that simply hasn't worked. To make that change, we need real skill. And since conversations that are in trouble have imbalance written all over them, we need good balance, too. In the next chapter, we'll start to find our balance, no matter how tough the going gets.

## Remember:

- Each side thinks the trouble in a tough conversation is the other side's fault, cancelling out blame on both sides.

- Our counterparts use an arsenal of thwarting ploys to get us to back off, to come out on top, or simply to get out of the conversation altogether.

- On our side, we want to avoid confrontation, but tough conversations drive us to get tangled in our own emotions, or swing from one extreme reaction to another, or stick to one old standby reaction—even when it doesn't work.

- Both sides might actually resist increasing their skill out of worry that something new won't work and will make the situation worse, or out of the sense that skill is really manipulation and good intentions should be enough.

- Nothing in a tough conversation is as simple as we hope.

## CHAPTER 4

# Rethinking What We Do

## *Finding Balance*

WE'VE SEEN WHAT makes us recoil when the trouble in a conversation dials up, whether because of an unexpected attack, thwarting ploys where we're vulnerable, our own emotional reactions, our counterpart's unreadable intentions, and worst by far, all of these coming at us at once. No wonder we respond to difficult conversations as we would to combat—they look dangerous.

But since we're not getting through these conversations the way we want to (and aren't getting the results we want, either), we need to do better. We don't have to face these conversations as though we're caught in the wheels of war. We can take a new look at the same conversations and rethink how to get where we want to go. We can let go of those familiar ideas, habits, and reactions we saw in chapters 2 and 3, since what's familiar doesn't help us. We can concede what we can't control (like unexpected developments and our counterparts themselves) and take hold of what we can control (like our strategy and how we handle our side). If we put in place approaches that don't depend on battle ploys, don't tie us up emotionally, and don't break down over misconceptions, we can change the conversations themselves.

First, a caution: difficult conversations themselves may be complicated, but we can't use a complicated system to bring them into balance. Under the pressure of the conversation, how would we remember what to do? Can we get a simple enough system though? Yes, we can. And the key to it starts with three-way respect: self-respect, respect for our counterpart, and a healthy respect for the problems in the landscape of the conversation itself.

It may seem odd to put such emphasis on respect here. For many of us, self-respect is a given. And if we do respect our counterpart, that, too, is a given—so why make a point of it? If we don't, then forcing respect sounds fake or too close to deference. Worse, forcing respect for a counterpart who doesn't respect us in return is odd, and forcing respect for a counterpart who is threatening, lying, or attacking us is ridiculous. And finally, respecting the conversation itself sounds suspiciously mystical. We will see, however, that the key to good practice is the combination of all three facets of respect working together.

## Self-respect: Your own good balance

"People with self-respect have a kind of moral nerve," author Joan Didion says. "The willingness to accept responsibility for one's own life—is the source from which self-respect springs." Didion thinks of self-respect as "a certain discipline, the sense that one lives by doing things one does not particularly want to do, by putting fears and doubts to one side . . . That kind of self-respect is a discipline, a habit of mind."[1]

When we're facing a difficult conversation, self-respect is a stance we take to brace against the pull of our own emotional reactions. The kind of self-respect we're talking about here is a long way from giving in to emotional strain. And it is not related to self-righteousness—the certainty that our interests, our positions, our views, our concerns are more valid or more worthy than those of our counterparts. We want to stay away from self-righteousness; it will drive a difficult conversation completely out of balance. Using Didion's habit of self-respect, we don't shrug and excuse ourselves by saying that our intentions were good, or that the trouble we're having is the counterpart's fault, or that we're not good at these conversations, even if all those things are true. Instead, this kind of self-respect lets us see, almost *makes* us see, that it's in our interest to move the conversation forward well. Keeping our eye on our interest protects us from reacting to whatever comes at us in the conversation. We are in control of the self-respect we bring to our side of the conversation.

That's important, because we can't count on the other side to bring respect for us. It will be wonderful if our counterpart does, but we have to deal with what we get.

This kind of self-respect—in tough situations, with people who are not, at the moment, cooperative—is a distinct leadership trait. How we handle ourselves whittles out our reputation, and our reputation is the most basic reason for bringing not only self-respect to these conversations, but respect for our counterpart, too.

## Respect for your counterpart

Regardless of what our counterparts are doing in a conversation, respect for them is in our interest because disrespect takes such a toll on reputations and relationships. Respect for our counterparts is a strong advantage to us. It's not a gift to them, and it's not contingent on their respecting us in return.

This kind of respect simply recognizes that our counterparts have interests and concerns that they think are valid. Respecting our counterparts, however, is not the same as agreeing with them or deferring to them.

When a conversation starts to degenerate, respecting our counterparts and their concerns isn't a familiar habit. We're more used to ignoring, downplaying, or misrepresenting their concerns or not being able to fathom them at all. But self-respect and respect for our counterpart feed into each other in a positive way. To handle a difficult conversation well, *both* are necessary.

How does that work in practice? What does a good balance between respect for the counterpart and self-respect look like? To find out, let's go back to a difficult conversation we've seen before, one that worked out badly the first time. Henry, the CEO, had rejected the new-style speech that Jennifer, his communications director, had prepared.

Recall that Henry had no trouble seeing one of his two big concerns: he wanted to keep his unscripted presentation style. It was, however, harder for him to look directly at his second problem: he would rather smooth over differences than address them head-on. Like a lot of us, Henry wanted to sidestep a tough conversation. What's wrong with that? Henry was already caught up in an issue that involved another person—Jennifer's unclear role as his communications director. The trouble in this case wasn't just Henry's preference for his old presentation style, but also the understandable fear of all the potential fallout that underlies difficult conversations themselves: a disagreement might turn into a battle of wills, one side or the other might lose face and get angry, good intentions might be misread, and worst of all, these problems might snarl together in a confusing mess of a conversation. Trying to sidestep fallout like this makes sense, but doesn't make it go away. In fact, as we saw, not talking didn't solve their problem; not talking exacerbated it.

But Henry did have another option: he could change on his side. Out of self-respect, he could bring to bear Didion's sense of doing what he doesn't particularly want to do. Just as he had acknowledged his own concern about presentations, Henry could have looked straight at the idea that Jennifer, whom he had hired and who was doing what he had hired her to do (albeit probably not as he had imagined), surely had concerns of her own around the presentations issue. He could actively respect that her concerns were in play, just as his were. That's not compromising—respecting them is not the same as giving in to them.

Henry could say to Jennifer, "I know you want to help me be a more polished speaker, and you're a professional. But my mind works better when I'm a little loose. Help me do even better what I'm already good at." Henry would find that comment a tolerable, nonconfrontational thing to say—after all, he said just that to the outside speechwriter. What if Jennifer doesn't meet him there, but pushes back? Henry doesn't have to react; he can stick to his balance between respecting her interests and respecting his own.

More important, though, is a by-product of Henry's new stance: his willingness to look at Jennifer's concerns, and talk to her about his own, changes the whole atmosphere of the conversation. It doesn't feel like a confrontation when Henry puts respect for the interests he recognizes on both sides in place of his usual pattern of avoidance.

Henry isn't the only one who could change what he was trying to do. Jennifer could, too. Respect in difficult conversations is an equal-opportunity practice. Jennifer could do on her side what Henry had done on his—acknowledge his concerns and talk about her own. Granted, Jennifer was not the senior person here. If the conversation did become a confrontation with a winner and a loser, she faced greater professional risk—and greater emotional fallout—than Henry did. Nevertheless, respect works just as well for a subordinate as it does for a CEO.

How would a turn to respect on Jennifer's side have made a difference? Step one: Jennifer knew her own two big concerns: on the one hand, she wanted to upgrade Henry's presentations for the higher-stakes events ahead, and on the other, she wanted to secure her status as the new communications director by getting Henry to use her ideas. Step two: Jennifer could look straight at the notion that Henry surely had interests on his side—without agreeing or giving in to them. And step three: Jennifer could openly acknowledge both and make her case. How would it sound in practice?

Jennifer could say to Henry, "I know you're famous for your on-your-feet remarks and comfortable with them, but your company is growing so fast that you need to grow as a speaker along with it. I can support you, Henry. I've brought a lot of experience with me." This time, Jennifer openly respected her strengths and skills at the same time that she openly respected Henry's. Even if it's clear to Jennifer that Henry was trying to avoid, well, *her*, she could raise the tricky issue between the two of them without the emotional blowout that pushed her to quit the first time around.

Bringing respect for our counterparts, their interests, and their concerns to a difficult conversation may not be a habit for us, even if, like Henry and Jennifer before their debacle, we agree that we respect, like, and admire our professional counterparts. With the combat mentality as our legacy, respect may not look wise or even possible. But in practice, it's more than possible— it's useful to us in a conversation that is running rapidly down-hill and taking us with it.

Henry and Jennifer are not home free. In fact, so far their differences are not resolved. But Henry's interest is now in play— he's talking about what he wants with the expert he hired. And instead of being shut out altogether, Jennifer's interest in Henry's success, and in her status and influence, is in play. Their conversation is headed forward in better shape. The suspicion, damage, and loss that colored the version of events in chapter 3 won't occur this time. And neither person has to worry about seeing the other in the office tomorrow.

## Respect for the conversation itself

Bringing self-respect to the conversation makes it easier to put respect for our counterpart's interests and concerns into play. And respecting their interests and concerns makes it easier to bring in our own. Together, respect and self-respect make a virtuous circle. Bringing them to the conversation won't end all our problems, but it will shift our focus. Instead of "the problem is me" or, more likely, "you are the problem," we see the problem as a feature of the conversational landscape itself. That shift alone— from thinking there's a problem in our counterpart to thinking there's a problem in the conversation—can turn around what we are trying to do by 180 degrees.

Self-respect and respect help us frame the problem between us and figure out how to talk about it. Meanwhile, respecting the landscape of a tough conversation assumes there will be problems ahead. Rather than put our heads down and start to plow through, we will do better to step back, take a satellite view, and think about the lay of the land. That is, think about the problems we are likely to encounter, and look for a good path through them.

I coached both Henry and Jennifer—separately—after their conversational breakdown. Each came to understand the role that respect could have played. In the aftermath of the conversation, Henry told me, "I admit that I hadn't wanted to get bogged down in how Jennifer felt. But when I look back on the way I handled it, I'm sorry I was so focused on just getting rid of the issue. I didn't have any trouble looking at my side of the 'scripted'/ 'unscripted' tussle. If I had looked at Jennifer's quite legitimate concerns about her standing in the company, too, I could have found a better track through the conversation. In fact, I wouldn't have gotten bogged down in the stuff on Jennifer's side—I would have *managed* that. Managing is what I do; that's what I'm good at. I could have gotten through the conversation with both of us intact."

When Jennifer took a new position in another company, she knew she didn't want any other difficult conversations to play out again the way hers and Henry's had. Thinking back on the conflict with Henry, she told me, "I looked at it as though my self-respect were on the line, but I *put* my self-respect on the line. All I could see at the time was a clear-cut case of win or lose. I couldn't step back and get any perspective on what we were doing, not what you call a 'satellite view.' But now, I can see how I could have worked it out better for both of us."

There's no question that Jennifer and Henry have the skills to respect themselves, respect each other, and look at a problem they want to solve. The trick is to put the skills into play when the pressure is on. When they—and we—do put them in play, the conversations start to look less like war and more like parkour. Instead of going down with the ship or bailing out of the conversation altogether, Henry and Jennifer could each look out for obstacles, knowing that some will be hidden, and bring skill to bear to make their way through the conversation. Either side could shift what he or she was trying to do.

It's often hard to separate out the strands of this new three-way respect. They weave together so smoothly that it can be hard to see where one ends and the next begins. Three-way respect takes us away from the combat mentality, lightens the emotional load of tough conversations, and allows for differences between intentions and perceptions on both sides. As a working attitude and a habit of mind, three-way respect is greater than the sum of its parts. It sets up a completely different starting point for tough conversations and becomes the base on which we build better balance into them.

## Balance within: The emotion problem

Because difficult conversations are emotionally loaded, the main challenge in finding balance within ourselves is stabilizing that emotional weight. We will always destabilize when we see only two extreme options, neither of them good—like the choice between "take the punch" and "retaliate." When Jennifer saw only the "take the punch or retaliate" choice after her non-conversation with Henry, she chose retaliation: she quit and took her staff with her.

If you get caught up in them, there are dozens of these choices that are simultaneously limited and extreme. Look at the questions people ask themselves: should I suffer in silence or blurt out? (What kind of lousy choice is that?) Bully or back down? Hang tough or go soft? This is the thinking that results in bad moves: After the Patriots' 2004 Super Bowl win, victory celebrations in Boston turned violent, leaving one person dead and another seriously injured. Mayor Thomas Menino believed that people would read his actions only as a choice between two extremes. When he talked about crowd-control efforts and how they would be discussed in the media, and said, "If you went hard, it would have been police brutality. Since we didn't quell the thing, we're being criticized for being soft."[2] If he believed he could only choose between the appearance of brutality and the appearance of softness, of course his outlook on any decision would be bleak.

But we're not hardwired for an either/or position in difficult conversations. We don't have to choose between brutal or soft, rational or emotional, win or lose, fight or back down. But what can we do to find balance instead?

## Moving in from the poles

Like Jennifer, Vivek, who was leading his first team meeting, saw the "retaliate or take the punch" choice. But unlike Jennifer, he didn't choose one extreme; he swung from one to the other. Twice he took the punch, letting it pass when Mack hassled him over a task decision, and then—boom—Vivek threw Mack out of the meeting, only to be criticized by his manager for his volatile temper.

Vivek used the "take it, take it . . . have a cow" technique, the only choices *he* could see. But good balance depends on finding middle ground between polar extremes. Middle ground is not only more effective in difficult conversations, it's also easier on us than trying to choose between "take it, take it" on the one hand and "have a cow" on the other. What else could Vivek have done?

As it happened, Vivek got it backward—he said nothing to each of Mack's *remarks* and then retaliated against Mack *himself*. But Vivek could have taken different tacks. Putting Mack's remarks on the whiteboard to acknowledge them, while continuing to stand by his own decision, is one tack. Telling Mack, "We don't agree on this, but it's where I came out when I weighed the pros and cons of how to handle the task" is another. Or Vivek could simply say, "I've got it," to a remark from Mack, and go on. Each of these tacks is halfway between "take it, take it" and "have a cow." But what about the undertone of challenge behind Mack's remarks? Doesn't Vivek have to deal with that?

No. Nothing raises the emotional temperature in a difficult conversation faster than a personal attack, as Vivek himself well knows, because it happened to him. Vivek had been caught off balance from the beginning, when Mack had razzed him and Vivek had not responded. But Vivek threw himself even farther out of balance by counterattacking. In front of the whole team, nervous and uncertain as he was, Vivek would have done better to find middle ground and stabilize himself than to follow Mack into the combat mentality. As it was, Vivek's reputation with his manager suffered more than it needed to.

### Expanding choices

Finding middle ground between extremes is one way to balance yourself; expanding the whole range of your choices is another. But it takes practice to get there.

In an academic meeting, David was stunned to hear Rachel laying claim to research findings she had learned from David himself. After the meeting, he complained to a friend, "I couldn't say anything. What was I going to do? Say in front of everybody, 'You stole my research'? If I had called her on it, I would have looked way out of line. No, I couldn't say anything at all. I had no choice."

David had the same old problem of seeing only two extremes: he could say nothing, or he could blurt out an accusation that looked "way out of line" to him. But there's a second problem of imbalance within us, and the key to seeing it is David's next remark: "I had no choice." Seeing only two possibilities and no viable choice between the two means that we haven't considered a full range of responses to begin with.

Why not? What makes our range of response appear so narrow? Here's the either/or predicament we find ourselves in: On the one hand, there's an unwritten principle in business that we check our feelings at the door. On the other hand, if we're being realistic, frustration, anger, and confusion are a package deal with a difficult conversation, and they provoke us. If we can't expand our range, our only choice is to pick one, and either the principle or the feelings will have to go. David checked his feelings at the door. (David could have gone the other way, however. Instead of thinking he had no choice but to say nothing, a different David might have believed that he *couldn't* check his feelings at the door: "I was angry, so I just called Rachel out for stealing my research. What could I do? That's just who I am." Sitting at either extreme, we get stuck on the idea that there are no other choices.)

What would it take to give David the sense that he did have better choices? If, instead of locking in on one narrow view, David could step back and take a satellite view of how to handle the spot he's in, he might change his question from "What was I going to do?" to "Who do I want to be?"

If he had asked himself, "Who do I want to be?" when Rachel laid claim to his research, David's answer would probably be close to this: "I want to be an academic researcher who knows and complies with the rules governing credit for research." With his answer, he has immediately expanded his range of responses to Rachel. The either/or straitjacket of a choice between saying nothing and blurting out an accusation is gone. He's neither stifling his emotion nor letting his emotions rip—he's stepping aside into another view of himself and of this conversation. It doesn't matter that other people are present. He's in balance within himself, and what he says will come from there. He might say, "Rachel, you'll want to credit those findings to my research with Professor Sullivan." He'll find his own words.

This time, even though he was still strongly provoked, David didn't simply react. His answer to "Who do you want to be?" was true and felt genuine to him, at the same time that it put some distance between him and the slight that got his back up. It put him in a balanced stance, like an athlete, ready to act rather than react. And he has brought his own self-respect to the conversation, which didn't—and didn't need to—come at the cost of disrespecting Rachel. His response to her—"Rachel, you'll want to credit those findings to my research with Professor Sullivan"— was neutral, not soft on her or deferential, not harsh or accusatory.

Why is it useful to David to bring respect for Rachel to this conversation, even though her behavior didn't particularly invite it and she wouldn't necessarily reciprocate? It's useful because there's a lot of room for mistakes in difficult conversations, and it's easier to recover from mistakes if you start from neutral ground. It's possible, for example, that David already had made a mistake unawares. Rachel's reply to him might be, "I did give you credit, David. It's in the handout." David could easily recover from his mistake if he spoke from a position of neutrality rather than disrespect.

And if Rachel had tried to benefit from David's research without giving him credit, or if she had made a professional error, she could back off if David didn't make her lose face and thereby push her to defend herself. But wouldn't David have *wanted* to make Rachel lose face, considering that he thought she was stealing his work? Well, this conversation was happening during a meeting, with other people watching. The public atmosphere would raise questions of relationship and reputation for him to consider. David still has the choice to assail Rachel for her theft, as he saw it, but remember that he had thought calling her on it would be "way out of line." He's in a better position to decide whether to attack her if he has "neutral" as one of his options. We want lots of choices, not just silence or attack.

Getting a better perspective on our own choices will give us better balance on our side. But we're not alone in these conversations, and finding balance between our side and our counterpart's is a much trickier business. The main trouble this time is seeing how the conversation looks to our counterpart or, for that matter, reading other people at all.

## Balance between the two sides

Most of us aren't particularly clairvoyant in difficult conversations, especially when confusion about intentions and perceptions runs in two directions: we can't read our counterparts, and at the same time, we don't know how they are reading us. In fact, this is how the "What's going on here?" type of hard talk in chapter 1 gets its start. Making matters much worse, our ability to read what's happening really plummets if the problem seems to be, well, *us*—but we can't tell why it's us.

Marta was a newcomer to a computer game start-up company. She was a committed gamer, had always wanted to work on games from the other side, and was ready to start. Hugh, the senior programmer who had guided her through orientation, liked her youthful intensity (that part of her reminded him of himself when he first started) and was glad to have someone like her on board. The day Marta started work in her first game group, Hugh patted her on the shoulder and said, "Good luck, kid. And speak up if you need something or have something to offer." Marta took him at his word. When she was working on a kids-market arithmetic game, and Coleman, one of the other programmers, produced a shooting gallery to teach kids how to subtract—by knocking off one Bambi after another with a semiautomatic weapon—Marta spoke up. "I don't think that's funny," she told Coleman. "Maybe your inner fourteen-year-old sent it in."

Later, Hugh took her aside, smiling, and said, "It's great that you say what you think." Then he stopped smiling and said, "You might want to cut people a little slack." The very next day, when Marta was passing Hugh and a group of programmers, she heard Hugh mutter something and all the guys laughed. "I don't even know what they were talking about," she reasoned to herself. But her mouth was dry and her palms were damp.

What happened here? Marta certainly didn't know. She couldn't interpret either Hugh's mixed message or his inconsistent behavior. Unfortunately, her best guide at the time was what *she* would intend if she were talking and acting like Hugh. But she didn't talk or act like that, so she was in the dark. It seemed to her that Hugh had first set her up and then put her down, even ridiculed her. She didn't know how she should take his comments, and just as bad, she didn't know how Hugh—or any of the other programmers—were taking her. Did they think she was pushy? Lacked a sense of humor?

It's unlikely that either Marta or Hugh would have described his or her own behavior in such derogatory terms. Marta saw herself as straightforward, and Hugh probably saw himself as diplomatic. And that's the problem: we see through our own eyes. What we see can be limited by who we are, but also by what seems normal where we live or work.

Hollywood producer Harvey Weinstein, who works in a culture where people are not always candid with one another, has earned a reputation for brutal frankness. He puts it this way: "Let me translate brutality in the movie industry: honesty. They say it's brutal. Yeah, it's brutal to tell the truth in an industry where everyone lies."[3] Is Weinstein brutal? Does everyone else lie? Even diametrically opposed points of view seem normal to those who hold them. But in a hard conversation, what's normal to one side can alienate the other. Each side thinks the other is handling their side wrong, and neither wants to close the gap between them. The conversation runs further and further out of balance, while each side holds the other to blame.

While Weinstein sounds convinced that he has nailed the malicious intent behind the behavior of his industry counterparts, Marta was not convinced that she knew Hugh's intentions or, for that matter, how he and the programmers were reading hers. But she also thought that knowing the intentions behind Hugh's remarks and the programmers' amusement was the only way she would know how to deal with them. She was caught in a bind—not knowing and yet believing that she needed to know in order to respond the right way. She still worked with all of them, and she had to do something. But what?

Before we go any further, let's be clear: we can't read our counterparts' intentions or know how they are reading ours. Marta's questions were not inconsequential: What was Hugh's take on her? What did he mean by his confusing comments? Were Hugh and she on the same page? And there is a good way to get her questions answered: She could *ask*. Marta could say to Hugh, "I've been thinking about how my remark to Coleman looked to you, and I realize that I don't know how you see it." That's the simplest, clearest, most neutral way for Marta to start dealing with the uncertainty between the two of them and, also important to her, to bring in her concern about the other programmers. It balances respect for her counterpart's point of view with self-respect. Neither side has been pushed down so the other side can be one up. In fact, it's beautiful. It's also uncommon.

### Bridging the perspective gap

We don't usually ask simply, clearly, and neutrally about our counterparts' intentions and perceptions, even to break an impasse like Marta's. Why not? Because of the way we look at hard conversations in the first place. Some of us see them from one pole, and some see them from its opposite (see figure 4-1).

At one pole, we don't need to know much about our counterpart's outlook, since we're controlling the conversation, anyway. At the other, we don't know what's going on, and we can't control

FIGURE 4-1

**Polar view of a hard conversation**

I'm in control; I know
what I'm doing

I'm not in control;
conversations
just happen to me

anything. At each end, there's a reason why asking about our counterpart's perspective looks like a bad idea.

If we're at the left pole, securely in control of the conversation, what's the point of asking about our counterpart's point of view? In fact, if we're in control, it can be disturbing to begin to see another's viewpoint. Not because we are so hostile to his viewpoint, but because we begin to understand it and don't know how to think through the changes that even guarded respect for that viewpoint would entail. Shouldn't we attack it? Will we have to give up our own point of view if we understand our counterpart's? Wouldn't he "win" the conversation, and we "lose"?

If we're at the right pole, we're at a loss, and there's a real chance that we will be a casualty of the conversation if we solicit the other side's point of view. What if she doesn't reciprocate? Won't the conversation get increasingly lopsided if we give credit for what's going on with our counterpart, but she won't give our side credit for what's going on with us? Even worse, if we admit that her point of view has any merit, will we give our counterpart ammunition that she'll use against us?

The reason that talking about intentions and perceptions looks like such a bad proposition has to do with that limited perspective on the conversation itself. Again, the narrow band of possibilities is misleading. A satellite view of a hard conversation reveals a lot more latitude than a limited, polar view does (figure 4-2).

"Two people who are not in accord now" is the balancing perspective we could take on the conversation itself. It would let Marta ask Hugh how her remarks looked to him. This kind of bal-

FIGURE 4-2

**Satellite view of a hard conversation**

| | | |
|---|---|---|
| I'm in control; I know what I'm doing | Two people who are not in accord now | I'm not in control; conversations just happen to me |

ancing perspective automatically includes self-respect and respect for the counterpart. And it has the benefit of being a much more accurate view of the possibilities in a difficult conversation.

To think about and take this balanced stance with our counterpart, we do have to get some inner balance, which we can't get from a position at either pole. The real beauty of working toward balance in difficult conversations, however, is that there's a reciprocating loop between balance within ourselves and balance between the two of us. The loop works like this: The more we focus on balance with our counterpart, the less we choke on our own worries. The less we choke on our worries, the more we can see and think about our counterpart's point of view, how this conversation could go, and what we can do to keep it in balance.

It sounds good, but how could Marta have come up with this when she was confused and upset enough to have sweaty palms? Maybe she couldn't. And, certainly, it wouldn't be a good time for a first try. Handling a hard conversation well is like performing CPR. When we need to do it, we are upset, the other person isn't helping, and we're unsure of the outcome. But we can do it if we have mastered the technique in advance. Marta wants to start bringing her mind in from the poles and looking for balance in hard conversations, and she wants to do it now.

We've seen how people can break old patterns and rethink balance within themselves, or rethink balance with their counterparts. And we've seen how people can step back from their conversations and take a satellite view to get a bigger and clearer picture of how the conversation itself is playing out. These skills help us overcome the habit of treating the conversation like a battlefield to be fought over or avoided.

## Moving through the conversational landscape

In parkour, traceurs who have a landscape to cross scrutinize it even as they move through it. In their eyes, an impediment is not much different from an advantage—they use whatever they come across to shape their path forward. For us, the landscape is where the conversation plays out. The problem between our side and our counterpart's side—the disagreement about a decision, the bad news, the criticism in front of other people, the threat and retaliation, the team meeting that fell apart—is part of the landscape. If our emotions are in our way, they are obstacles in the landscape, too, as are thwarting ploys. Misconceptions are pitfalls there. The relationship between us and our counterpart also plays out in the landscape, whether we preserve the relationship, strengthen it, or damage it.

Focusing on the landscape takes some of the pressure off the two players in the conversation. This focus helps us, especially when we're on our feet, to keep the conversation less about the people facing each other—less about us versus them—and more about the obstacles and advantages in our path, even when the two sides have a bad track record for talking about a problem that will not go away.

Teddy and Livingston were two colleagues with that kind of a track record. Teddy was a star software-solutions salesman, terrific in the field, but a misery to everyone who had to back him up in operations. Livingston was his beleaguered manager. Although he needed Teddy, Livingston knew Teddy was very difficult. Livingston also knew that he himself had been too forgiving of Teddy in the past. But now the people in operations were up in arms, and again, Livingston had to deal with Teddy.

Livingston usually started conversations with Teddy by praising his performance with customers, at length and in detail, then

saying "but," and then bringing up the problem of internal relations. Teddy had always heard the praise and dismissed the problem, claiming that the operations people were slow and mistake-
prone. One time, Livingston had swung to the opposite tack, but
that had been a fiasco. He had come down a lot harder, and
Teddy had been outraged and threatening.

This time, Livingston changed his focus. Instead of looking at
*Teddy* as the problem, as he usually did, he saw the problem between them as a feature of the conversational landscape. An ob-
stacle, to be sure, but one he could talk about with a traceur's
"What have we got here?" attitude. And that's how he did talk
about it. He said to Teddy, "With customers, you're the best. In-
house, you're not. That gives me a problem; in fact, it gives both
of us a problem. What are we going to do?"

That sounds good. Nevertheless, Teddy responded true to
form. He emphasized his own prowess and disparaged operations.
"I'm out there working miraculous deals," Teddy ranted. "And
then some stick-in-the mud wants to slow me down because this
deal isn't just like the last one and that might be a problem for
them! They like old deals, from the fifties, before there was software to sell!" For the first time, Livingston saw Teddy's comeback as a recognizable feature of the conversational landscape.
And for the first time, it didn't push him off balance. Livingston
didn't swing from a soft extreme to a tough extreme, as he had
before. He stayed neutral, respecting Teddy, respecting himself,
and focused on the problem between them.

"I like it when you do a good deal. They like it, too. When you
send them a hazy report, though, they wish they could read your
mind, but they can't. There have been some missteps before—sometimes in what you promised a client and sometimes in what they
thought you did from the sketchy details they got. That doesn't
work for you, or for them, or for me. What are we going to do?"

Not surprisingly, it was an effort for Livingston to stay focused and neutral. He did it, but pretty doggedly. Later he said,
"First it seemed monotonous to stay the course and not react to

Teddy. But then it got interesting—Teddy stopped fighting me and he seemed to stop expecting me to back off. It just took the steam out of him not to have much to fight against. Things happened differently this time."

## Opening new possibilities

When you stop seeing limited choices for your own behavior and you stop reacting to your counterpart, you begin to see recognizable patterns in the landscape. Even better, you begin to see what your counterpart is doing and how you can meet that or neutralize it. You might even begin to see why your counterpart is acting the way he or she is. How would all this work in the situations we've seen before in this chapter? When we can detach the problem from the counterpart and look at it as a feature of a larger landscape, we can address the problem with a tough mind. That's different from getting tough with the counterpart and, in difficult conversations, probably less familiar. We're used to sticking what's wrong in the conversation onto the counterpart because we're used to the combat model. Much less often, we will take the problem away from the counterpart and stick it onto ourselves— either to preempt an attack by blaming ourselves in the first place or to spare a counterpart if we don't think he can handle the conversation. That's the way boyfriends used to break up with you: "It isn't you; it's me." But we don't have to limit ourselves to picking out which of the two of us is the problem.

In fact, there's no good reason to set ourselves up with a choice between being tough or soft on our counterparts or on ourselves. The sales manager, Livingston, was used to only two choices: handling Teddy with kid gloves or taking the gloves off. But once the novelty of looking at the problem as a feature of the landscape wore off, he found it much easier to respect Teddy and respect himself. When he put respect in place for the two of them, Livingston could defend with a tough mind the important concerns of the operations people who backed up Teddy's work. He could thump consistently on the problem in the landscape in a way he couldn't if there was no distinction between the problem and his counterpart. It's a small change of focus with a big payoff.

But how does it actually sound when people talk about a problem in the landscape? Here's how it sounded in Teddy's case. Speaking of the people in operations, Teddy said to Livingston, "They are precise—they have to be—and accurate, and they pay attention to the letter of the law. When we're in conflict, I can find them inflexible and unimaginative, but they are always willing to get things done. It can seem, though, as if they think I'm intentionally doing things incorrectly." That was the first time Livingston had heard Teddy speak so genuinely about the people he worked with, without self-promotion getting in the way.

The problem here isn't solved for Livingston and Teddy. But the conversation sounds normal, even though the subject was tough and relationships were in danger. The tenor of the conversations is hopeful. The personal attacking and sidestepping have given way to a clear focus on obstacles in the landscape—and ways to work with them.

Specifically, what was different in the new version? Livingston had shifted to respecting Teddy, respecting himself, and respecting the problem between them. He had stopped minimizing, and he had stopped exaggerating altogether. He didn't appease Teddy or provoke him. He didn't try to take control in the conversation— and make Teddy resist him—but he didn't back off, either. Instead, Livingston took a satellite view of the situation and saw Teddy and himself in a landscape populated with clients and support staff alike, and the two of them had a problem in common.

All the conversations in this chapter have begun to sound normal, although not easy. The people are not ignoring trouble with a counterpart in order to have a normal conversation, and they are not nervously faking normality even when faced with all the signs of a tough conversation. Instead, they are taking steps to bring a difficult conversation into balance. The conversations are beginning to *be* more normal, even though emotions are still prickly, problems remain, and perceptions don't agree.

There's one more critically important aspect to rethinking what we're trying to do. In each of these cases, one person changed what he or she was doing unilaterally and thereby changed the nature and direction of the conversation itself. If we're suffering from the kinds of problems people here have faced, we too can make changes to our conversations single-handedly. Let's see how.

## Remember:

- We need a simple system to handle tough conversations, and three-way respect is its basis.

- Self-respect helps us stabilize in the face of our own emotional reactions. It brings us in from the extreme emotional poles at the same time that it expands our choices for handling ourselves well.

- Respect for our counterpart is a willingness on our side to look at our counterpart's interests and concerns—not necessarily agreeing with them, and not deferring to them. Respect trades asking about those interests for guessing at them, fighting them, or avoiding them.

- Self-respect and respect form a synergistic loop. Together they determine our reputation and our relationships.

- Respect for the problem places all that we're struggling with into the landscape of the conversation itself. It lets us step back and take a satellite view of the way our tough conversation is playing out. The conversation is no longer a battlefield, but a course of obstacles through which we move.

## CHAPTER 5

# Acting Unilaterally

OST PEOPLE think that there are two necessary ingredients for good results in difficult conversations: trust and mutual respect. If we and our counterparts trust and respect each other, the thinking goes, then even difficult conversations will work out. If we do have trust and respect between us, however, we are in a "soft" difficult conversation. Much as anyone would prefer to have any difficult conversation in an atmosphere of trust and mutual respect, we can't require them up front. A few good outcomes in hard conversations might get us and our counterparts *to* a place where we trust and respect each other, but realistically, we are not likely to start there. Unfortunately, in "hard" or even toxic talks, at least one side does not bring trust, or does not bring respect, to the conversation.

So we need to look for what we can do unilaterally to change the track of a hard conversation. We do want respect in the conversation, and mutual respect is better, of course, but we can't control the "mutual" part. If we insist on "respect from your side for respect from mine," we give our counterparts a lot of power to thwart us. All they have to do is not show us respect, and the conversation will stall. We can work better if we bring the respect and the self-respect to the conversation ourselves.

We want to think like parkour traceurs. If traceurs were moving through a difficult conversation, they would be looking very clearly at where they were and where they could move, where their counterparts were and were likely to move, and where they themselves wanted to arrive and what was in the way of getting there. Traceurs have a lucid and independent "What have we got here?" attitude toward obstacles and pathways alike. And that's what we want. This is very far from disregarding our counterparts; on the contrary, it explicitly considers them. But it does not imagine that we and our counterparts are beginning with a solid, trusting relationship.

What would it look like to find a way through the landscape of a difficult conversation, acting unilaterally?

## The Red Team and the Green Team

Nathan and Eileen were both managers in a rapidly growing health-care company. The team Eileen headed—we'll call it the Red Team—was new and, frankly, underperforming. To make matters worse, the quality of work that came out of Nathan's team—the Green Team—depended on what came through to them from Red. So Green had a real stake in Red's performance. During a meeting of their own, Nathan's Green Team vented about the problems they had because Eileen's Red Team wasn't up to speed. Later, through the grapevine, Eileen heard about that meeting. Embarrassed and angry, she confronted Nathan. "From now on," she said, "I want a representative from my team at any meeting of yours where you talk about us."

Nathan thought that this was a ridiculous, high-handed demand on Eileen's part. But he also knew that if he couldn't resolve this conflict between them, matters between the teams would worsen.

Even so, on his feet, he could think of only two things to do: be stubborn and say no to Eileen's demand, or back down and agree to it. We've seen this before: with his thinking riveted on how to react to Eileen, Nathan was headed straight to choosing between two dead-end poles.

But then Nathan decided to see what he could do unilaterally to put the conversation on a better track. Instead of responding to the specifics of Eileen's demand as though he were facing a quiz with only two possible answers, Nathan began to think in terms of questions like these: How could he get through the conversation well? Where did he want to come out? What could he do in the face of obstacles? With these parkour-type questions for his conversation with Eileen in mind, Nathan found he could step back and see the conversation taking a recognizable shape, although not a good one. But the narrow choice for him between "be stubborn" and "break down" was no longer on the map.

Looking at the landscape of the conversation before him, he said to Eileen, "I don't want to push back on your point. At the same time, I don't think it will look right to my team to agree with you, either." Nathan simply talked about what he saw. He then went on to talk about the different ways of looking at what the makeup of team meetings should be when contentious issues were under discussion. He thought aloud about the advantages and disadvantages of different configurations. Soon Eileen was joining in, adding her own past experience with team meetings. The conversation between them went forward from there. While the problem between the two teams had yet to be solved, the conversation between Eileen and Nathan didn't escalate and it didn't degenerate. That could be even more important than any solution they do find, because, as managers, they need a functioning relationship—even when they're both angry—in order to work out their teams' problems.

The big change here for Nathan was that he talked neutrally with Eileen about their disagreement, in a balanced conversation. Once Nathan had a good experience under his belt, he wasn't going to trade in his new focus on the landscape for his old tendency to react to every counterpart and ploy or to assume that a hard conversation was automatically the same as a fight. But even Nathan was surprised by how much he gained. He stopped focusing on the poles in his conversations and, at the same time, expanded the range of good possibilities in difficult conversation—not just on his side, but between his counterpart and him, too. And he did it unilaterally; he and Eileen were not working jointly to put the conversation on a better track, although Eileen left her own track once a better one presented itself.

## Putting unilateral change to work

In fact, in all the tough conversations we have met so far, the revisions have been made unilaterally. Henry, the CEO with a speech to make, had previously had one key concern: to smooth over differences with Jennifer, his communications director (although not only with her), rather than confront them. When Henry stepped back and looked at the conversation with change in mind, he could see that he had limited himself to two dismal extremes. But he could unilaterally shift the direction of the conversation he dreaded by finding middle ground (figure 5-1).

Here he could ask for help with what he really wanted— "Help me do even better what I'm already good at"—rather than avoid the conversation, clash with Jennifer, or defer to her preference. How did he get from avoidance to an open, balanced difference of opinion between his communications director and himself? Henry unilaterally changed what he was trying to do. If Jennifer had wanted to make a unilateral change on her side, she could, too—"Your company is growing so fast that you need to

FIGURE 5-1

**Finding middle ground unilaterally**

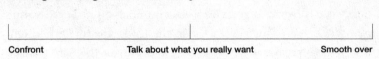

| Confront | Talk about what you really want | Smooth over |

grow as a speaker along with it. I can support you, Henry." She would not be avoiding, clashing, or deferring, either.

When Marta, the new computer programmer, revised her approach to senior programmer Hugh, she said, "I've been thinking about how what I said to Coleman looked to you, and I realize that I don't know how you see it." That was the most balanced way for Marta to start dealing with the uncertainty between the two of them. It was not mutual balance, however, but unilateral balance. Yet neither side was pushed down so that the other side could be pumped up.

Livingston, too—the manager who had a long and rocky history of hard conversations with star salesman Teddy about his poor rapport with the operations staff—was able to step back and take a satellite view of their conversation. He stopped looking at Teddy as the problem, the way he usually did, and started seeing the problem with operations as a feature in the landscape of the conversation itself: "With customers, you're the best. In-house, you're not. That gives me a problem; in fact, it gives both of us a problem. What are we going to do?" Livingston put the problem in the landscape—and kept it there—unilaterally, even when Teddy reverted to the old, familiar oppositional mode. And when Livingston did keep the problem in the landscape, the range of responses available both to him and to Teddy opened up a lot wider.

In each of these examples, one person changed what he or she was doing, single-handedly. One side shifted stance in the conversation, which shifted the whole conversation. Moving conversations this way doesn't have to be a joint effort. We can do it ourselves. In fact, we want to put ourselves in position to work out difficult conversations rather than have them happen to us. It's the difference between diving and falling into the water. There is skill, on the one hand, and on the other hand, there's an accident, one that hurts a lot.

## Change within: Handling emotions unilaterally

It isn't necessary *not* to be angry, *not* to be nervous, or *not* to be frustrated to handle hard talks well—if we weren't having any emotional reaction, we probably wouldn't think it was hard to begin with. However, it is possible to be just as frustrated, just as nervous, and just as angry, but more competent. We need an approach that doesn't deny the strong current of emotion going on, but doesn't go whole hog into it, either.

The emotional weight of a difficult conversation can destabilize us, so it helps to see clearly where we're vulnerable and how we react. We usually seem to be blindsided by a hard conversation that we aren't expecting, although we ought to expect it, since we've suffered through our share of tough conversations already. We don't have to wait until a difficult conversation is in our face to start working on balance within ourselves. In fact, it's much better not to wait. The best time to do a self-assessment of what we struggle with most is when a problem conversation is *not* looming.

Unfortunately, instead of checking out our vulnerabilities, most of us tend to build strategies around our strengths. In situations we can control, that's a good idea. But in difficult conversations, attempts to control generally backfire, and our counterpart's reactions are never something we can control. If we concentrate on our strengths, and a tough conversation presses on a vulnerable point, which it invariably does, we're exposed. We have to learn to balance our emotions ourselves, even if our counterpart triggers them.

Shifting our focus for the moment away from Nathan and toward Eileen in the quarrel between the Red Team and the Green

Team, let's hear how Eileen described her concerns over giving Nathan's Green Team the bad news about delays on her own Red Team: "I'd be okay if I could stick with the announcement and didn't have to go to dialogue." In terms of self-assessment, she knew she was all right saying her piece (that's familiar to many of us), but she didn't look closely enough at her worry that, in the face of angry reactions, she would crumble. As a result, she repeatedly made the same mistake. Instead of working out how to deal with angry reactions, she tried to avoid them by doing all the talking and then leaving the room, cutting off the Green Team's responses altogether. That's understandable, but it increased her counterparts' anger and frustration and gave her a reputation for being unreasonable and demeaning.

If this is what Eileen suffers now, then we want to look at what she can do—right now, on her own—to find better balance. If Eileen could strike a balance within herself, she could make a unilateral change, as Nathan did. But in her case, she wants to change the way she handles her own vulnerabilities. Eileen doesn't seem to lack self-awareness, but she did seem to lack a way to deal with the vulnerability she knew she had. If she were to step back and take a satellite view of her defensive (and offensive) way of handling an awkward conversation, she would see that she consistently takes a position destined to throw any conversation off balance. Then, if she could look straight at her worry about falling apart if people got angry, she could acknowledge it and, at the same time, ask herself, "Who do I want to be?" She might answer, "The manager of a new team in an embarrassing situation who is determined to solve problems with the least possible fallout for others and for my own team." That would be true, and a much more balanced place to stand within herself as she faced a hard conversation about her team's performance.

Eileen—and all of us—can use this self-respecting, emotionally balanced approach unilaterally. That's important, because we can't count on our counterparts to bring skill, balance, or respect to the conversation on their side.

## Change between: Seeing our counterparts' perspective

When we bring self-awareness and self-respect together—and use them—we improve our own balance. But because we aren't alone in this conversation, self-awareness and self-respect aren't enough. Certainly, we can build strategies for handling our own emotional triggers, and we should. At the same time, though, we also want strategies for dealing with both our own viewpoint and our counterpart's, together. In tough conversations, the two viewpoints probably don't match. Even so, we need to give equal weight to respecting our counterpart's concerns, although not necessarily agreeing with them. That means looking for balance with our counterpart as well as within ourselves. And while our own emotional imbalance is usually pretty evident, a perspective imbalance between us and our counterpart—and how to handle it—can be harder to read.

This step, respecting our counterparts' concerns, can be counterintuitive for three reasons. First, most of us are trying to reduce the number of things we have to think about in loaded conversations. Like Eileen, we don't want to add one more piece when we're already overwhelmed.

Second, giving equal weight to our counterparts' concerns doesn't make sense if they won't acknowledge ours. We're just handing them extra ballast for their own positions.

And third, guessing doesn't work well. We're not psychic; we don't know what our counterparts think or will do. And too many times, we've been in conversations with people who know we have a different point of view, are certain they know what ours is, and are dead wrong.

Bernard Cardinal Law, archbishop of the Catholic Diocese of Boston, for example, badly misestimated his counterparts' point of view concerning the issue of child sex abuse by priests. He needed, and perhaps wanted, to apologize for the devastating crises brought to the church on his watch. But he repeatedly apologized for the wrong thing: Cardinal Law didn't apologize for the crimes of abuse, but for not knowing sooner what he later learned. The people in his church did not think that was the worst harm; that was not their perspective at all.

But Cardinal Law's mistake was not that he misguessed his counterparts' perspective but that he was working on a defensive strategy, not a balanced strategy. In fact, with a defensive strategy, it would not be useful to him to acknowledge another perspective. With a balanced strategy, it would be.

We don't want to complicate a hard conversation by adding one more thing to do. Rather, we want to avoid oversimplifying it by sidestepping a part of the conversation that has a huge influence on it, whether we want it to or not. We don't want to defer to our counterpart's point of view at the expense of our own, but to balance the two. We don't want to presume the other side's perspective, insistently, right or wrong, in a way that bolsters our own. But we do want to recognize that that they have one, think about it, and bring it out into the air. Remember that Marta, the computer programmer in chapter 4, was very nervous about Hugh's and the other programmers' angle on how she had handled herself. At the same time, she didn't know what that angle was. To stand a chance of a balanced conversation, she brought it up— simply asked about it—unilaterally.

At the same time, we don't have to depend on our counterpart to ask us back. Just as we can consider our counterpart's point of view—or ask about it—unilaterally, so too can we talk about our own viewpoint without taking turns. It would be great if our counterpart considered our point of view or asked about it in return—if Hugh had said the equivalent to Marta—but it isn't necessary. We can balance respect for our counterpart's point of view and self-respect on our own. That's what Nathan, the Green Team's manager, did when he said to Eileen, "I don't want to push back on your point. At the same time, I don't think it will look right to my team to agree with you, either."

So, even if it makes us uneasy, we want to make our best assessment of the counterpart's point of view in this conversation. What is our counterpart likely to think the problem is here? Are we and our counterpart on the same page?

Carl, the software product manager who had Ernesto taken off a project that Ernesto was heavily invested in, knew the answer to the second question—no—but he didn't do anything with it.

Remember that Carl and Ernesto were the two managers on a software product team who had a blow-up when Carl took Ernesto off the project because Ernesto worked on it at the expense of other teammates and other projects. Looking back at that conversation, recall that Carl knew Ernesto would have a strong and frustrated response, both to the decision and to how it was made. Yet in the conversation itself, Carl disregarded Ernesto's perspective. Instead, Carl countered Ernesto's strong reaction with reasoning that worked for his own perspective: "We've gone over this again and again. You always agree that you can, and will, manage your time better." That tack had worked poorly, and Carl wanted to rethink what he was doing, because he wanted a better outcome. What could he change?

Before the conversation with Ernesto began, Carl could have made his best assessment of Ernesto's point of view. If he had asked himself, "What is Ernesto likely to think the problem is here? Are he and I going to be on the same page?" and if he had looked straight at the interests he knew Ernesto had, Carl might have said to himself, or to Abby, his CEO, "We're hitting Ernesto with a stick here. Can we give him a carrot, too?" And certainly, they could have come up with the carrot.

If Carl had worked for balance between himself and Ernesto, would that mean that he was no longer having a difficult conversation? No. What was happening was very hard. Carl would still know that what he had to say would not be well received. And Carl's decision itself would still be painful to Ernesto and anger him. But the conversation between them would go better, with less damage to the two sides.

## Change in the landscape of the conversation

When the going is hard, we are often unaware that there's a conversation unfolding in a recognizable way at all. But we could be aware. When we're better balanced within ourselves, we stop polarizing our own behavior. When we're working toward balance with our counterparts, we stop simply reacting to them. Even better, we begin to see what our counterpart is doing and how we can meet that or neutralize it. We might even begin to see why our counterpart is acting the way she is. That's when we can step back and see the landscape of the conversation as though it were spread out before us. To see how that would play out in a familiar difficult conversation, let's look again at Nathan and Eileen, managers of the health-care company's Green Team and Red Team.

When Nathan stopped reacting personally and took, instead, a satellite view of their conversation, what he saw Eileen doing made some sense to him, even though her demand itself was unreasonable: Eileen needed to protect herself and her team from embarrassment. She couldn't deny her team's slip-ups. But she couldn't admit them, and save face too, when Nathan's team was bad-mouthing her team behind closed doors and then leaking their remarks. Eileen's demand was a smoke screen of sorts—she had to make some kind of objection.

Nathan was still annoyed by Eileen's high-handed demand, but at the same time, he could see past his reaction. He said, "I felt like a pool player after the break. It was like I was walking around the table, reading the layout, and I could see different possibilities. Mine, and Eileen's, too." Although Nathan was thinking pool, unilaterally he looked at the landscape of the conversation with a traceur's eye, seeing where he wanted to move and what was in the way of getting there. Possibilities were clear, and he started to think more than react.

Consequently, the first reasonable conversation with Eileen had a ripple effect on their two teams. When Nathan and Eileen

called their ceasefire, their teams talked together without sniping. Someone on Eileen's Red Team said to Nathan, "When you're
working on deadline, you can get pushy without realizing it."
Another said, "I feel like there's a perception that we don't work
as hard, or that we're not as diligent." And then someone on
Nathan's Green Team said, "A solution needs to be found. I'm
afraid that blame and fault-finding will be the focus."

All the players in the conversations in this chapter, not just
Nathan, were unilaterally looking for ways to put their conversations on a better track. These people did not begin with trusting
and respectful relationships with their counterparts, and the
truth is that they may not have reached full trust and respect by
the end of the conversations, either. But the conversations were
working, not failing. Relationships were beginning to balance,
not worsen. And the people in them were handling their hard
talks with new competence.

## New thinking over old stumbling blocks

Change is hard. But so are conversations that are collapsing and
taking us down with them. There's a lot of room for improvement in how we handle difficult conversations, and these chapters shine a light on good ways to begin to handle them better.

Changing how we handle difficult conversations can seem a little like changing a golf swing—ninety things we have to remember when the pressure is on. But in fact, it's more like being a kid
when someone notices that we would be better off with glasses.
For the first time, we can actually read what's on the blackboard—
everything is clearer and makes more sense. We feel better. And
we look cool, too.

If we put our attention on working toward balance—within
ourselves, between the two of us in the conversation, and in the
landscape of the conversation itself—we stand a good chance of
protecting our reputations and our relationships. And we need

and want both of these, even if right this moment we would just as soon forget about both and let 'er rip. When we can replace a gut reaction with a balanced response, we are on our way to being genuinely competent at handling difficult conversations well, which is a much better deal than conversational failure, however cathartic one gut-reaction moment of the failure might be.

We will need all the competence we can get, because difficult conversations still won't be trouble free. The playing field is not always level, and our counterpart might have the high ground. The thwarting ploys can come thick and fast. And the counterpart's intentions can be ruthless. The next chapter looks at the first of the greatest and most serious pitfalls in finding good balance in difficult conversations—power challenges.

## Remember:

- We will bring self-respect and respect for our counterpart to the conversation unilaterally, because we can't depend on working jointly with our counterpart in an atmosphere of trust and mutual respect.

- We will change what we're doing on our side to talk neutrally about our disagreement in a balanced conversation.

- We will handle an emotionally charged and complex conversation with competence, not denial.

## CHAPTER 6

# Conversational Warfare and the Combat Mentality

J ANE, A DISTRIBUTION COORDINATOR for a printing company, went pale with anxiety when she realized that a colleague who was now on vacation had bungled the details of an order for Gary, a major customer. Jane was twenty-six, and this was her first serious job. She admired her manager, Deirdre, who was a little older, a little distant, successful with customers, and always busy. Jane wanted to impress Deirdre and hoped one day to emulate her cool, competent manner. But today, with Gary's order all wrong, she couldn't.

Gary was already testy over an earlier delay in receiving the packets of material that he had carefully created for a security conference, but Jane knew that he didn't yet know how badly the order had been muddled. So she spent the afternoon and evening on the phone, trying to recall the faulty conference packets and replace them. The shippers said it might be too late to intercept the delivery, but they would do what they could. Although Jane worked very late, making corrections to the order for a new rush shipment, she didn't finish before she finally went home to get some sleep.

When Jane sat down at her desk the next morning, the first thing she saw was an e-mail from Deirdre, telling Jane to come to her office as soon as she got in. Jane was extremely nervous, and as it turned out, with good cause. The delivery had not been stopped in time. Gary now had the packets, but too few of them. The materials were out of order, and in some cases, pages were missing. Seeing the mistakes, Gary had angrily called Deirdre from the conference venue.

Now Deirdre was angry, too. "You put me in a terrible spot," she told Jane. "I didn't even know what Gary was talking about. He yelled at me because we screwed up his order. Then he actually had to bring me up to speed himself, and then he yelled some more. I sounded clueless and incompetent. What were you thinking?"

Without giving Jane a chance to answer, Deirdre got louder and angrier. "You've embarrassed me with Gary, and he's furious. This will go further up the line, unless he stops doing business with us altogether. And if it does go further upstairs, it will come home to me, not you. Your name isn't on this disaster; mine is."

Drawn with fatigue, Jane shrank in her seat as Deirdre laid out the enormity of the problem. The more Deirdre spoke, the worse her own situation looked to her. She was soon incensed.

"That you didn't show more competence with a major order is one thing," Deirdre said. "That you're so self-important that you won't keep me informed is much worse. I have too much invested here to be hung out to dry by you."

"I'm so sorry," Jane said. "You had already left when I realized the packets were wrong. It wasn't my mistake, but I thought I could straighten it out. And I was going to tell you first thing this morning, but Gary called first."

By now, Deirdre was livid. "Stop it. Stop making excuses. I do have a phone, and you could have called me. If you're going to take chances with my professional reputation, you need to do better than that."

Then Jane cracked. "How can you talk to me this way?" she shot back, her voice rising. "I said I was sorry. I'm not making excuses. I didn't mean to keep you out of the loop, and I tried hard to correct a mistake I didn't even make. What do you want me to say?"

As Jane and Deirdre glared at each other, Deirdre's phone rang and she turned to answer it. With her back to Jane and ice in her voice, Deirdre said, "Watch yourself. I won't forget this."

## Combat rules of the war zone

Jane and Deirdre have plenty of problems in this painful and destructive conversation, but they also have a big problem that isn't *in* the conversation itself at all, but is pushing it and shaping it: the combat mentality. This mentality can kick into gear when a conversation gets tough, and turn the conversation toxic. When a conversation no longer seems simply hard, but feels threatening, confusing, and unpredictable, it starts to look like combat. In this case, Deirdre appeared to have gone to war, and Jane certainly appeared to be under attack. Each of them then imposed the combat model and its rules on the conversation as they saw it. The combat model won't get them—or anyone else— good results, but the more we work from the combat mentality, the more accustomed to it and invested in it we become. And combat always brings to the fore issues of power, control, and win-or-lose, zero-sum thinking (half of the six basic types of difficult conversations in chapter 1 are concerned with combat and its characteristics). In the combat model, the issue of power is the first we confront.

## Power: One-down, one-up, and both sides

Once the combat mentality clicks into place, we begin to think that power—who has more, who has less—will determine the conversation's outcome. We're not always right about that, but power does influence the approach many of us will take in tough conversations. It doesn't matter whether we take the perspective of someone one-down in power, like Jane, or someone one-up, like Deirdre, or both. This is combat, and power rules.

### The one-down view

Within the combat model, people one-down in power generally have a straightforward point of view: if we think we can't win, we don't engage. It's foolish, even dangerous, to have a difficult conversation when the balance of power is against us. But of course, too often a difficult conversation is sprung on us when we don't expect it. As Jane found out, it can be impossible to dodge.

When we can't avoid a tough conversation, the combat model has another rule: if we think we can't win and we're forced to engage, make ourselves a small target. Keep a tight lid on what we say and show, because, as happened to Jane, anything we say can be turned against us. Even with that rule in mind, however, it's hard to know whether maybe we should push back if we feel cornered, which is what Jane finally tried.

In practice, each rule of combat conversation seems firm, but together, the rules are confusing and contradictory. It's very hard to know what to do. And more to the point, whether keeping a lid on or pushing back, people one-down aren't so much participating in the conversation as they are reacting to someone one-up. In this case, Deirdre was leading, and Jane was just trying to keep up—until Jane snapped.

### The one-up view

It's not always obvious to the person one-down, but people one-up worry, too, or they ought to, because when they fail at difficult conversations, they pay a big price. At the moment she was talking to Jane, Deirdre was too angry and embarrassed to concern herself with any potential cost to her of the confrontation.

But she might have taken a lesson from what happened to Colin, a senior government-agency administrator who had some tough my-way-or-the-highway conversations with staff members about his new program priorities. He was satisfied with his handling of those conversations until he found himself, first, in a 360-degree review and, next, out of a job himself. In fact, studies show that the two most common traits of top executives who derail—like Colin—are brittle relationships and inflexibility: the executives alienate the people they work with and can't adjust their style.[1] Their power can boomerang against them if a conversation goes badly and word gets out, although like Colin, they may not see that coming.

### Ratcheting up control

Difficult conversation is threatening to both sides, one-up and one-down. When we're one-down, we feel threatened *by* power. When we're one-up, we feel a threat *to* our power. In the combat model, everyone caught up in a difficult conversation feels that a conversation going wrong is not sufficiently controlled. If they had more control, both sides believe, they could make it work out.

If we're one-up and a conversation is going badly, we believe we're not using our power advantage *enough* to control what's happening. That's how it looked to Jack, the CEO of his family's company in chapter 1. He didn't back Mike, his handpicked senior vice president and longtime friend, when Mike was thoroughly dressed down by other senior managers in front of Jack. Why not? Despite his top position of power in the company, Jack felt challenged by the confrontation with Gus (the veteran manager who handed his resignation to Jack and then led the attack on Mike). When Jack felt challenged, genuinely substantive issues—such as the effectiveness of his new leadership vision—gave way to issues of power and control, and Jack reacted accordingly. He picked his battle, however. Jack didn't go after the veteran managers. He ratcheted up his control later—in single combat with his already deeply wounded friend, Mike.

If we're one-down, we try to control *ourselves*, particularly any expression of emotion. We don't want to appear weak or defiant, or afraid. That's a tough act to pull off, especially if, in fact, we do feel weak, defiant, or afraid. So our first choice when facing a hard talk with someone one-up is to avoid it. That way, we won't get snarled up in what we feel and what we think we should show. But if we can't avoid it and we also can't control ourselves well enough, then we might lose control altogether and come out swinging, as both Mike and Jane did. Whichever happens, the conversation *itself* seems out of control.

And yet, isn't it obvious to try for control at times like this? If we take a combat view toward difficult conversations, the answer is yes. It's equally obvious for our counterpart to try to resist. What happens next? One side tries to increase control, and the other increases resistance. Control like this more often worsens the conversation than it helps.

### Both one-up and one-down: The zero-sum view

Whether we're one-up or one-down, we take the same view of still another rule of combat conversation: there will be a winner and a loser. On the one hand, whoever is one-up is the expected winning candidate. But on the other, neither side—including the one-down—wants the other to win at his or her expense. Ray, a labor union rep, made that point clear when he talked with managers who probably had the edge in power: "I used to attack all the time. If someone made a good comment for the other side, I had to knock it down so they wouldn't get ahead."

This is zero-sum thinking in action—the fear that anything the other person gets comes at our expense. Like Ray, we can't afford to allow our counterparts *any* kind of gain, or they will get the upper hand and we will lose ground. But zero-sum thinking and the fear of losing are definitely not limited to the person one-down in power.

For example, both zero-sum thinking and the fear of losing colored the tense relationship between Francis, a new manager at a North Carolina botanical garden, and Yvonne, a long-standing employee responsible for an exotic collection. At forty-five, Yvonne was reserved and independent-minded; she had been instrumental in building and maintaining a well-regarded collection of plants and had worked autonomously for several years. Nevertheless, Francis, at thirty-one, was gregarious and ambitious and wanted to enforce a closer reporting relationship as part of a general administrative realignment. Although Yvonne resisted close oversight of any kind, she loved her work. When she realized that her resistance was widely known and likely to cost her her job, she made a concerted effort to repair the damage to her relationship with Francis and with other senior staff.

As those other relationships began to improve, however, instead of being pleased by Yvonne's progress, Francis tightened the screws on her. He was increasingly critical of her, even in public. Things came to a head at a reception, when Francis belittled Yvonne's accomplishments in front of some donors. He walked up to a group of donors talking about greenhouses with Yvonne, listened for a moment, and then interjected, with a patronizing smile, "Yvonne has been a good little housekeeper for us." Francis was unaware that the donors had known Yvonne for years and had a high regard for her careful work. There was a distinct murmur of protest from the donors—they were indignant on Yvonne's behalf. Later, they complained to the botanical garden's director about Francis.

Yvonne posed no challenge at all to her boss's position—she was barely out of the doghouse, shakily holding on to her job, and not on a management track to begin with—but Francis saw her small gain in stature as threatening to his own. His zero-sum thinking made him suspect that any improvement on Yvonne's side, even a slight increase in respect, would come at his expense. This isn't completely logical, but it is how zero-sum thinking works.

## Combat rules in conflict: Might or right?

Why do we stick to a combat model, with such a shaky set of rules, whether or not it works for us? In part, because we don't have another model. With few alternatives apparent to most people, the combat model has three points in its favor:

- **IT'S SIMPLE.** If the answer to the question "Who will 'win' a conversation?" is "Whoever is one-up in power," then a complicated and highly charged communication problem is, at least, reduced to something simple that we can get our minds around.

- **IT'S FAMILIAR.** If a tough conversation plays out on television, the script invariably turns it into a show-down—one side wins, the other takes a bullet. We see it all the time.

- **IT DOESN'T TAKE MUCH SKILL.** If there are only two possible outcomes—we have more power and we win, or we have less and we lose—difficult conversations that go badly are like natural disasters, and we can just throw up our hands: there's not much we can do.

But, as H. L. Mencken said, "For every complex problem, there is a solution that is simple, neat, and wrong." What's wrong with the combat model of tough conversations? The first big problem is that even with the combat model, there's more to difficult conversations than a power imbalance, and we know it. When we peel back the superficial layer of power rules (if you think you can't win, don't engage; if you're one-down, make yourself a small target; if you're one-up, you win), we find a different, incompatible rule: "I am a good guy and I am in the right, so if my counterpart resists me, the wrong is on his side." And the worse the conversation gets, the more likely it is that one side or the other will turn to it. We're still battling, but the rules just changed—from might to right. How does that happen? How does right come into a scene that used to be determined by might? (See "The Three Stages of Battle.")

It happens when, at some point, the conversation crosses a line. Something new appears to be at risk, something more fundamentally important than a power position: our self-respect. We are *people* involved in these conversations, not just entities in respective

## The three stages of battle

We don't always expect our difficult conversations to go so wrong. But if we can bear to recall our worst experiences, we'll recognize the usual stages of battle:

### Stage one

We go into the conversation with optimism and self-assurance, the best intentions, or at least the conviction that we're right. We tell ourselves, "This will be quick and bloodless—it's not really going to be a war."

### Stage two

Our counterparts are not following the script. They dodge us, push back, raise the emotional temperature, or simply think that *they* are right. Soon we realize, "This is worse than I thought. I have to bring more control or resistance to bear so I don't lose."

### Stage three

Afterward, when we review the wreckage of the conversation, we draw our conclusion: "That was horrible. But what happened was inevitable and not my fault."

With the combat model, everything that would actually help us— skill, respect, balance in the conversation—has been forgotten or shut out altogether.

power positions. In nearly every example we've seen so far, self-respect eventually trumped the one-up and one-down rules. As soon as that happens, simple power rules are out the window.

### The David and Goliath rule

For every time we buy into the old, familiar power rules—if we have more, we win; if we have less, we lose—there's another time we buy into the David and Goliath rule of combat.

The David and Goliath rule focuses on the good guy, the guy in the right, the one with angels on his side. This slant on who ought to win feels true to us as flesh-and-blood people, not as inhabitants of power positions alone. But there's a problem. In difficult conversations, as in every tough situation, *no one* identifies with Goliath. Everyone, including Jane's manager, Deirdre, feels like David—a good guy up against it. So how does the David and Goliath rule help us with the conversation? Not well.

We're tangled in contradictory rules of combat here, even though we want rules in the first place in order to make these conversations feel more manageable. But much of the time, we *can't* follow them. Why not?

There are two reasons. First, difficult conversations are too complicated for the rules. Even the question of who's one-up and who's one-down can be unclear. When there's tension between two senior vice presidents, who's one-up? Who's one-up in a wrangle between an IT expert and a director in another department? Who's one-up in a bitter disagreement between a top-tier athlete's agent and a team owner? In hundreds of confrontations, how can we consistently apply power-based rules when it's hard to know who has more power? In the same way, if both sides think they are in the right, how can the David and Goliath rule possibly work out?

### David didn't follow the conventional rules

The second reason why the rules of combat don't consistently work is both basic and more significant: tough conversations, in fact, are *not* combat. We overlaid the war model on conversations when we were confused and anxious and didn't know what else to do. And this is the reason that an entirely different message in the David and Goliath story is the big one for us: David didn't get caught up in conventional rules about power or winning and losing. He put his attention on strategy and skill.

Instead of getting caught up in the conventional combat view of tough conversations, what we too really want is better strategy and skill. The combat mentality first slips in when there's a strategy vacuum. We want to put our attention on changing what we're *trying* to do, and the first step is to move away from the combat model of difficult conversations altogether and to put strategy in its place.

Good strategy is thinking, planning, preparing, and, sometimes, practicing ahead of time, not just in the heat of the moment, what we want to do and where we want to go in a hard talk. Our strategy is the raw material we must take into a tough conversation with a counterpart who is unlikely to see the situation the way we do. It's our realistic estimate of where we're likely to find ourselves struggling, and it's our preparation for dealing with that. Working from strategy, we assume there will be problems ahead and we anticipate how to handle them. At the same time, we expect to be taken by surprise—but strategy gives us useful places to focus when we are surprised. Strategy is smart, and it has our experience behind it.

In the face of tough conversations, good strategy is a habit of thinking, not a script. We think about where the conversation is likely to get snarled, and we plan how we might move if it does. Having good strategy doesn't mean we won't have bad moments; it just helps us think well when we do.

## Lifting the fog of war

With good strategy as an alternative, it just isn't useful to think of difficult conversations as power contests or rights contests, with one side winning and one losing, even though those are simple and familiar views. None of this reasoning helps us find balance with our counterpart in a difficult conversation—the kind of balance we found in chapter 4. Power contests and rights contests don't help us talk through tough problems in uncomfortable situations or preserve good working relationships with people we can't eliminate from our lives. Contests like these teach us to be adversaries, and that's the wrong exercise. In difficult conversations, the combat model simply works badly and is a liability to us. So, we'll drop it and pick up a new approach that starts with good strategy and ends with good balance.

But we can't count on the other person to drop the combat model, too. We must break the mold unilaterally.

Working unilaterally, we will put respect and self-respect at the forefront of conversations that are going badly. It's unexpected, but it's possible to bring respect to a conversation even when we are angry with our counterparts, when we suspect they are not being honest with us, or when the conversation is being undermined in some other way. Putting respect up front does not put us one-down or weaken us. And it can be done even if our counterparts are disrespecting us. The idea that if we bring respect and they bring a combat mentality, they'll wipe the floor with us is as shaky a proposition as the other conversational warfare rules.

On our own, we're going to work through a tough conversation more strategically. Thinking strategically lets us see how we could move and how our counterpart could move—even how our counterpart is likely to move. It lets us think forward rather than react to what has already happened, or react to our counterpart, or react to how we feel. When, instead of reacting, we make a strategic move, we can rebalance a conversation, even one that is badly off the rails, and get it moving forward again.

# Remember:

- When we're caught in the combat mentality, we think there are power rules, including David and Goliath rules, that determine who will "win"—but they are not rules of nature.

- Instead of getting caught up in conventional rules about winning and losing, we will focus on strategy and skill.

- Good strategy is thinking and planning what we want to do and where we want to go in the conversation, while assuming we'll face obstacles.

## CHAPTER 7

# Out of Combat

## *Changing the Game*

O N THE DAY JACKIE, a manager in the auditing department of a bank that had been made much larger by a recent merger, had a review scheduled with Ross, who was one of her new reports, she was nervous. The bank had firmed up its performance evaluations to make them more specific and fine-grained.

Through the grapevine, Jackie had heard that Ross was known to be ambitious and quick to challenge any feedback that didn't serve his professional forward motion. She had also heard that Ross's auditing skills were more advanced than his interpersonal skills. Apparently, Ross had a superior manner that alienated people in the departments he audited. Because audits are admittedly a little hard to take, the managers chafed when they thought he condescended to them while criticizing their procedures. This was a bit hazy—Jackie hadn't heard this from an offended person directly, but word had gotten around to her.

Evidently, no one had ever said anything to Ross directly about an attitude problem, because criticism made him defensive. In fact, the managers at Ross's old independent bank avoided confronting Ross with his weaknesses—they were auditors, not personal-style critics.

Unlike Ross, but like his former managers, Jackie was non-confrontational—she was drawn to auditing because it was quiet and she could spend most of her time with numbers. But she took the grooming of younger colleagues seriously. If Ross wanted to progress, he needed to take a more tactful approach with managers who resisted his auditing conclusions.

It was important to Jackie to be fair, and she wanted this to be a constructive review. She'd looked over his previous reviews, but with the new evaluation format and the feedback she'd gotten from the department's clients, and her own assessment of Ross's work, Ross would not receive the same number of "exceeds expectations" ratings that he had received in the past. Nevertheless, Ross would see a good salary increase, proportionally more than Jackie had gotten when she was at his stage.

"Ross, your auditing skills are stellar and I'm impressed," Jackie began. "This is our first review, but you have a good track record. I can see how well your previous managers thought of you."

"Thanks, Jackie," Ross replied. "I'm pretty pleased myself." Off Ross went in that direction, filling Jackie in on his successes. Jackie listened, nodding, smiling, and agreeing.

"But there is one other thing I'd like to mention," Jackie tried. Still, Ross continued with his opinion of the high quality of his work. On that tack, Jackie wasn't making progress on the attitude problem at all. It seemed she had no choice but to drop the niceness and hit the point head on. "I've heard," she said, "that some department managers are unhappy with the way you come across when you're making your recommendations. They think you're kind of cocky and superior. You need to work on your interpersonal skills. That's going to be one of my 'going forward' recommendations in this evaluation."

Ross gave Jackie a look she couldn't read—was it veiled hostility? He denied any difficulty. Then he pushed back, "You review me, but you don't see me day to day. In fact, I don't think you know anything firsthand about my work." He twisted the conversation around to attack Jackie—he even questioned her competence. "You have a lot more new reports since the merger, not just me. Are you feeling a little overwhelmed, Jackie? In over your head?"

Jackie was taken aback by the confrontation and thoroughly stumped by Ross's twists. She lost track of what she was trying to say as she reacted to Ross, defending herself. Then she tried to regroup and decided to meet Ross halfway. "We're getting off track. Let's see what recommendations I can make that work for both of us." But this played right into the approach Ross had used in business school, and he conceded nothing to her. In his eyes, it looked as if Jackie were beginning to back down, and if he pushed her even harder, she would back down even more.

By that point, Jackie had had enough. This was no longer a disagreement about box scores on an evaluation; Ross was undermining her authority. She took the gloves off. "I need to tell you frankly that it's unacceptable that managers think you try to bully them in their own departments. And this very conversation is giving me the evidence I need. I'm disappointed in you."

"Bully people?" Ross shot back. "The way you're doing now? You're doing to me exactly what you accuse me of, and at greater cost because you can hurt my career."

Jackie and Ross were at an impasse. Ross said he wasn't satisfied with the review and he would take it up elsewhere. He left. Afterward, Jackie told her own managing partner everything. The partner commiserated with her and told her, "This happens, Jackie. There's not much you can do. Just give him a vanilla review. We have a grapevine that communicates anything people really need to know about his performance." That same grapevine, of course, carries messages about Jackie and the trouble she has managing up-and-coming auditors.

## What happened here?

Everything but the kitchen sink hit Jackie in this difficult performance review, and Ross fared no better. Jackie and Ross didn't see—or predict—the problems here, but we have spotted them.

To begin with, Jackie did know she had an uncomfortable conversation ahead—the "I have bad news for you" type—because she had to address the awkward issue of Ross's attitude problem. But Jackie did not foresee that the review would morph from bad news into almost every other basic type of difficult conversation. She faced "What's going on here?" when Ross responded so negatively to her recommendation. That in turn escalated to "I'm being attacked!" which is especially hard for nonconfrontational people like Jackie. Even that wasn't all. Before Jackie and Ross reached an impasse, she had been affronted by "You're challenging my power" and stumped by "You win/I lose."

This may seem like piling on, but difficult conversations are typically a complex mix. If the conversation goes on for a while, as this one did, it can run all over the place. Nevertheless, Jackie is senior to Ross, and neither she nor Ross came to the review with bad intentions. So why did this conversation go so badly for her? For them both?

Jackie had no strategy for a difficult conversation. Yes, she had prepared the topics she wanted to cover in the performance review—she had a grasp of the problem with Ross's attitude and some supporting information there, and she had a scoring plan for the review with a figure in mind for Ross's salary increase. She had a commitment to fairness. And she had what she considered a constructive opening. But Jackie put her head in the sand as to how the conversation was likely to go. She had no strategy for a conversation that wasn't going to be congenial, one in which Ross would refuse to accept her points or her conclusions. When the conversation began to tilt wildly out of balance, she floundered. She found herself reacting to Ross and his thwarting ploys. She found herself trying to bargain with him and failing. But she never found herself implementing a strategy to deal with what was happening in the conversation itself.

Without a good strategy for a hard talk, Jackie fell into the combat conversation routine. Characteristically, when the conversation didn't go in the direction she had intended, because Ross stuck to the topic of his successes, Jackie took firmer control of its path. But when that served only to heat up the conversation by antagonizing Ross, she couldn't work out a way to cool it down. Jackie's situation steadily worsened. She wasn't winning; in fact, she was losing ground in the face of Ross's attacks. The conversation now felt like full-blown, zero-sum combat, so Jackie herself—nonconfrontational Jackie—raised the ante, asserting her authority in order to win. As pitched battles will do, this one ultimately degenerated into losses on both sides.

This pattern is much too common. Jackie isn't alone in finding a conversation perilous and then finding herself sinking into conversational warfare. It happened to Deirdre and Jane, too, Ross himself, and most of the other people in this book. It was hard on everyone's reputation, not to mention their relationships. There must be something that improves the odds of lowering damage and raising outcomes.

## Strategic thinking

To get away from conversational warfare—power and rights contests, zero-sum thinking, and win-or-lose battles for control—and into the kind of strategic thinking that will get us to a balanced conversation with a chance of a good outcome, what should we aim for? More specifically, what is good strategy for the unpredictable? What can we do when we don't know what lies ahead?

Before we focus in on the steps we're going to take—which we will do when we look at tactics—we want to stand back and take a long-distance, strategic look at our hard talk, the way we would look at a parkour course. We want to know, on our side, both where we're headed and where this conversation is coming from. With that in mind, here are three places to start creating strategy: First, work out a *preferred outcome*. Second, imagine a *preferred working relationship* with our counterpart. Third, identify the *interference*—that is, whatever is getting in the way.

### Working out a preferred outcome

Our *preferred outcome* is our answer to the question "Where do I want to get in this conversation?" Thinking through our preferred outcome serves two purposes. First, it helps us keep forward motion through the screwy patterns of a difficult conversation. If Ross is taking Jackie off on tangents, if he is trying to get her to back off her point, even if he's using some other thwarting ploy, then an awareness of her preferred outcome can hold Jackie on course and protect her from simply following or reacting to him.

Second, thinking through our preferred outcome protects us from aiming for an unrealistic outcome, which badly undermines good strategy in hard talks. If Jackie had thought to ask herself, "What's my preferred outcome in Ross's performance review?" she might have seen that her first preferred outcome ("I want Ross to recognize that he has an attitude problem and agree to my recommendation that he work on his interpersonal skill") was unrealistic. Given what Jackie knew about Ross's history with the problem, that first pass at a preferred outcome is also naive. Not only is Jackie closing her eyes to the resistance Ross is likely to show, but she's also putting her own preferred outcome entirely in Ross's hands—for Jackie to get the outcome she wants, *he* has to recognize the problem and *he* has to agree to the recommendation. That's not independent strategy, and in difficult conversations, that's not a good idea. (See "What Do You Want?" for more on preferred outcome.)

It would have been much better if Jackie had scrutinized this first preferred outcome and said to herself, "I don't think that's going to happen." Then she could have aimed for something more realistic. She might have lowered the bar and broken the conversation into two parts: the first part to raise the attitude issue and the second to work on it with Ross when he wasn't taken by surprise. Wouldn't that just give Ross time to collect more ammunition against her? It might. But being startled tends to heighten a person's sense of being attacked. And if Jackie's recommendation is valid, it will stand. Given what happened when Ross *was* taken by surprise, removing surprise from the conversation is not likely to make the conversation worse.

With that kind of realistic frame of mind, Jackie would have been better prepared for the whole conversation and Ross's likely response. In fact, because she's nonconfrontational by nature, Jackie might have done more to help herself get to her preferred outcome in the review. She might have gotten advice and assistance in advance. She might even have practiced the conversation with a trusted colleague.

We settle on our preferred outcome unilaterally. We have to, because we're doing this in advance of the conversation. But our preferred outcome will never be a dictator's decision—"I am now determining how this conversation will come out"—because we've given up the power-and-control combat model, recognizing that the conversation involves two people who are probably not entirely on the same page. *Preferred outcome* is where we want to get, where we think we can get, and where we're trying to get. Once we hear our counterpart's concerns, we might adjust our preferred outcome. That's fine. But we should have one going in.

### Imagining a preferred working relationship

Side by side with preferred outcome, the second strategic issue to focus on up front is *preferred working relationship*. Thinking this through ahead of time would have helped Jackie when her conversation soured.

## What do you want?

S arah, a senior vice president in an advertising agency, met with me to talk about a complicated, difficult conversation she faced with her director. It involved managing up, addressing issues across departments, scrutinizing interactions with clients—just about everything. And given the personalities involved, all kinds of things could spell trouble. It took her a long time to describe the problem. At a pause, I asked her, "What do you want?"

Sarah flashed me a look of irritation and then described in greater detail the complicated nature of her problem, additional ramifications, and why the conversation would be so difficult. I asked questions to help me clarify what she was talking about, and then I said, "Sarah, I do need to back up a couple of steps and ask you again what you want. Where are you trying to get in this upcoming conversation? What's your preferred outcome for it?"

This time Sarah looked at me more closely with less exasperation and said, "I am so caught up in this that I can't even think of an answer to your question."

The next time we spoke, she said, "I was thinking about your question—what do I want?—and my question back to you is, How many answers can I give?"

In a difficult conversation, it is much easier—and more effective—to talk about a good thing we want and what's interfering with it now than it is to talk about what's wrong with our counterpart. That counterpart might put up his own preferred working relationship, but for the two of us to be talking about what a good working relationship looks like is better than talking against each other. It keeps us out of combat mode. But isn't this the very kind of soft, overly positive idea that got Jackie into trouble with her opening? No, because the third strategic step—

Of course, she could give as many answers as she wanted, and they could be as contradictory and incompatible as she wanted—for now. She laughed, because she did have a lot of contradictory answers. Even that was a real breakthrough for Sarah strategically. It was much better for her to confront the incompatible outcomes she wanted in advance of the conversation with her director. It helped her sort out her priorities and prepare to address conflicting interests if they came up, which they would. Part of what she wanted she couldn't get, and it helped to just plain admit it. She stopped floundering in her prep and focused on the forward motion of the upcoming conversation itself: where it might go, what opposition she would be likely to face, and how to respond to the opposition.

Afterward, Sarah reported that her strategy prep had given her a satellite view of the conversation as it unfolded: "I found myself thinking, 'It makes sense that my director just got angry; I see why he just accused me of not having my facts straight. I get why he's backing off his last remark now.' It looked more like game plays—some simple, some hard—than like a hurricane with all kinds of lethal things flying at me from everywhere."

identifying what's interfering with the relationship we want—builds in balance, which Jackie didn't have and couldn't find.

People know what makes a good working relationship—whether it's with their bosses, colleagues, subordinates, or clients. People also think that the characteristics of a good working relationship are obvious and universal, but that's not true. It's worth telling our counterpart in a difficult conversation what our *preferred working relationship* is—how we want the relationship to be. That is, after all, coloring our side of the conversation. Not only may our counterpart not know what our idea of a good working relationship is because it's not obvious, but he may not agree with it because it's not universal.

For example, in the same bank where Jackie and Ross worked, several young branch auditors, like Julie, spent all their time on the road as a team. All of them said that the most important characteristic of any preferred working relationship was "good interpersonal relations." That made sense. On the road, they worked in the branch office together, stayed in the same hotel, went to the same gym, ate together—they practically lived in one another's pockets. Getting along was crucial.

But back at the home office, their colleagues did not put such a premium on interpersonal relations. "It's not that they don't matter," said Derek, who worked almost exclusively at bank headquarters. "But I go home to my family at night, and as much as I can, I leave the office behind. The main thing for me is the quality of someone's work and their reliability." The difference between Julie's priority and Derek's does not matter as long as all is well. But we can see that if Derek were critical of Julie, she would be likely to try to smooth out the relationship between them. Derek, on the other hand, with a focus on due dates and wanting Julie to give extra time to what he needs from her, might dismiss her effort as beside the point. Julie is likely to misread him, and off they go into a damaged conversation.

### Identifying the interference

In planning strategy, *interference* is the companion category to preferred working relationship: we know what our preferred relationship is, so why don't we have it in this conversation with this counterpart? What is interfering with the relationship we want? What's conflicting with our ideal? (Some of that we may know, and some we may not.)

Notice the slant that the two categories together—preferred working relationship and interference—put on our strategy. They ask not what is amiss between us and our counterpart, but between us and our own preferences. This strategic slant helps for three reasons. First, it lets us think about the problem with our counterpart as a discrepancy between the situation we have and the one we want, without disparaging our counterpart or denigrating ourselves. Second, it lets us raise the topic of the working relationship we're aiming for, without assuming that our counterpart does, or ought to, agree with us. And third, because it is our own independent view, it is not open to refutation from our counterpart, although she may offer an alternative view. We're not telling our counterpart what's wrong with her, or even dictating what's wrong between us. Instead, we're talking about something nonprovocative. With such a strategic slant, our counterpart is not encouraged to defend or attack.

What would this kind of strategy look like for Jackie? To begin, this much we know about Jackie's *preferred working relationship* with Ross: Jackie wanted to be helpful to Ross because he reported to her and she took the advancement of her reports seriously. Moreover, she favored constructive conversation and solutions that appear fair to both sides.

Now, looking at *interference*, we recall that from the information Jackie gathered before the review, she knew three things that would probably interfere with her preferred relationship with Ross during the review. First, Ross would be likely to challenge her suggestions if they didn't contribute to his advancement. Second, he was defensive about criticism. Third, he was likely to be surprised and resistant to comments about his personal skills and unlikely to agree with those comments.

In the review, when they hit the roughest patch—Ross's attitude with clients—how would Jackie's plan to use preferred working relationship and interference have played out?

Jackie might have said to Ross, "We haven't worked together long, so I want you to know how important it is to me professionally to help my reports advance. I want this to be a constructive review that looks fair to both of us. That gives me a problem because I want to talk about a tough issue that I don't think you've heard about before. I think it's going to be hard for you to hear."

Here, Jackie has put together the package of her *preferred work-ing relationship* and *interference* that speaks directly to what she reasonably believes will be the difficult part of this conversation. She hasn't softened and she hasn't escalated. She has been respect-ful of Ross, herself, and the difficulty between them.

## Strategic balance

Jackie wants balance here. Typically, when they're talking, peo-ple stop after preferred working relationship and before interfer-ence, to stay on a good note. But in the original conversation, Jackie had too much trouble getting the bad news out after her good-news opening. And we saw Ross's reaction to the way she handled it. At best, he might have seen Jackie's approach as bait and switch; at worst, he would think Jackie was a hypocrite. It will always be awkward and unsettling on both sides if we're well down the trail on good news and then we fall—or are pushed—off a cliff into bad news. Balance between preferred working relationship and interference can prevent that.

In looking at how good strategy applies, as we're doing here, we are looking back at what *did* happen to see what *could have* happened if Jackie and Ross had strategy in mind. But we're not depending on hindsight to repair Jackie and Ross's performance review. Jackie did not need to foresee how the review would ulti-mately implode to figure out that it might. Like a Boy Scout, Jackie needed to Be Prepared. And in fact, her inkling that Ross would resist didn't even have to be correct—if he didn't push back, nothing lost.

Surprisingly, thinking through our preferred outcome and looking in advance at the combination of preferred working rela-tionship and interference together help bring balance to the con-versation, even though it looks as though we're tipping toward ourselves. (But see "Beware False Balance" to make sure that true balance has been brought to the conversation.) Knowing our preferred outcome helps balance us so that we don't blank out or simply react if our counterpart is provocative. It gives us something to hold on to and a sense of direction.

In a similar way, identifying both our preferred working relationship and interferences with it helps with respect and self-respect. Together, those two points of strategy give us a way to frame and talk about a difficult matter, a way that is not bruising, but is not soft either. Preferred working relationship and interferences can bring us and our counterpart into balance because they invite the counterpart to respond in kind, meeting our preferred outcome with his own, placing his preferred working relationship and interferences next to ours.

## Beware false balance

Jackie wanted Ross to accept her criticism of his attitude with clients, which to Ross looked like giving in. Ross wanted Jackie to retract her criticism, which to Jackie would be backing down. Jackie did try to break out of that loop and get the conversation back into balance: she offered to meet Ross halfway when she proposed they come up with recommendations together. Why didn't that work?

For compromise to work, it has to be mutual. Compromise looks like the balance point on the control span—with dominance at one pole and deference at the other. But surprisingly, in difficult conversation, compromise as a balance point is a false lead. If Ross doesn't agree to meet Jackie there, she can't bring balance to this conversation by offering to compromise unilaterally. What looked to Jackie like a mature effort to find middle ground looked to Ross like Jackie's backing down, which was exactly what he was hoping for in his struggle for control of the conversation. In his eyes, if Jackie could back down a little, she could back down more. They weren't on the same page, and Jackie was stuck again.

Because neither Jackie nor Ross had a strategy, their conversation was personally adversarial—a zero-sum battle over who would win and who would lose. Strategy, particularly thinking though a preferred outcome and a preferred working relationship, offsets that kind of personal boxing match and focuses on addressing what people want and what they can get, instead of who's got the upper hand.

Does planning strategy like this seem hopelessly cerebral for a hot disagreement like the one between Jackie and Ross? Certainly, it is human nature to have strong feelings and to act on them. But it's also human nature to think. Strategy helps us respond with our head instead of our gut. In difficult conversations, humans are good with their brains engaged.

I began this section with the observation that strategy helps answer the question "What can we do when we don't know what's ahead of us?" An equally important question is this one: "Is bringing balance to the conversation desirable, not to mention possible, if our counterpart is acting like Jackie or Ross?" The answer to both is yes.

First, even by the standards of combat conversation, Jackie and Ross had a poor outcome: there was no winner in the performance review; there were two losers. Of course, it's desirable to do better than that. And by the standards of professional conduct and advancement, the outcome for both of them was also poor. Their reporting relationship was badly damaged, and reputations on both sides were harmed. It's desirable to do better than that, too.

But, second, is it possible? If our counterpart won't cooperate, how can we bring balance on our own?

## Three-way respect

Because a combat conversation is a struggle between winning and losing, it *has* to be unbalanced. We want to—we're going to—

change the game away from the combat model of difficult conversation to one with better odds of working well with less damage. The heart of the new model is a new relationship that can be described succinctly: "We are two full-grown human beings in a difficult conversation. You're one of them. I'm one of them. We're in this together."

Our new, balanced relationship moves away from an emphasis on power positions in difficult conversations—not in order to wish away power or to switch it from one side to the other, but to move power from the foreground to the background. What comes to the fore? Respect.

We'll move away from trying to figure out how to control our counterparts or resist their control, or how to win and not lose, or whether to escalate or back down. We'll scrap those tense models of opposition and replace them with respect and self-respect. But how do these changes from combat to respect actually play out in a difficult conversation? Gunnar and Marshall, in the next paragraphs, show what it looks like in practice.

Senior management in a large and busy Oregon hospital wanted to change its emergency room procedures, which would require doctors to shift their elective surgery scheduling. When Gunnar, a senior vice president of operations, told Marshall, a senior surgeon, what needed to happen, Marshall folded his arms and told Gunnar bluntly, "We're doctors; we don't like people telling us what to do."

Gunnar winced. He had not intended to start a head-butting battle of power and control, but he could see why Marshall had taken the stand he did. Gunnar dropped the point for the moment.

Later—after planning strategy—he came back to Marshall and tried again. "You and your staff have struggled for too long with backed-up, frantic emergency rooms," Gunnar said. "It's a problem on our side, too—timing in the emergency room is also a management issue. We want to try a new approach, but it has to be a joint approach. If it doesn't work on your side and on our side, it won't work for emergency room patients, either."

This time the senior surgeon unfolded his arms and replied, "As I said, we're doctors and we don't like people telling us what to do. But we're also team players and we believe in teamwork. I don't know what we'll end up with, but let's put your plan on the table and see what we've got."

In his second effort, Gunnar openly respected his counterpart, himself, and the problem between them. Where those three parts connect is the balance point, and he took the conversation there. That's what changed the game.

The surgeons had stood on their scheduling prerogative for years, not wanting to give in. But unlike a combat conversation, a conversation with three-way respect doesn't have anything to do with one side's giving in to the other. It has to do with two full-grown people with a problem between them. It's balanced. When Gunnar moved unilaterally to respect and self-respect, Marshall had little to push against. By taking the tension out of the combat, Gunnar brought the conversation into balance. And as it happened, the scheduling change he and Marshall worked out not only helped the emergency room timing, but also caused no inconvenience for the surgeons.

What does three-way respect mean in our own difficult conversations? And how can we cover so much ground unilaterally in these conversations?

### Respecting our counterpart

Because we are so used to the idea of battles for control in conversations that have turned toxic, respect for our counterpart is harder to embrace in those very tough conversations than it is in "softer" difficult conversations. But respect toward our counterpart is a strategy—a working attitude—not necessarily a heartfelt sentiment. We're not talking about affection or admiration, although if they are present, they will do our work for us.

Of course, we cannot count on respect reciprocity, because we can't control what our counterpart does, and the chances are good that our counterpart is caught in a combat mentality of her own. Why would we want to bring respect to a conversation in which respect is not returned?

Out of self-interest, first. When we recognize that we cannot compel our counterpart to the outcome we want without real harm to our relationship and reputation, we can stop and move to respect, where the conversational track record is better.

Out of self-protection, second. Respecting our counterpart, we are much less vulnerable to avoidance, gut reactions, escalation, or pushback. Those are all choices, too, but their prospects for success are small.

Out of self-respect, third. As Joan Didion put it, "one lives by doing things one does not particularly want to do." If our counterpart is disrespecting us, we could disrespect him back and be no worse than he is. But we would be worse than *we* want to be.

We want to bring a strategy of respect to the conversation, unilaterally. Even assuming that our conversation is difficult because we and our counterpart have a damaged working relationship, and a history of bad blood, and our counterpart is the offender this time, we start on our side. (But see "Emergency Strategy for When We're on the Receiving End" for a viewpoint from the other side.) If we wait for our counterpart to behave better before we change what we do, I don't think it will work, or at best our wait may be a long one. Jackie did not get respect from Ross when she waited for it; Gunnar, the hospital senior vice president, didn't wait.

Why is respect toward the counterpart so rare and hard to put into play in difficult conversations? For some people, the idea of respect is simply off the radar. They don't have respect as a habit and never offer it. Those people are often baffled when a conversation takes a wrong turn, even if they use questionable tactics themselves, and they always blame the counterpart when it happens.

Still others have whole categories of people they don't respect. These people use disrespect as a ploy. A school board member once asked my help in preparing for contract negotiations with his teachers union. Negotiations didn't seem to go as well for

# Emergency strategy for when we're on the receiving end

Ross's situation was different from Jackie's. For him, the bad news in the review came up unexpectedly. What's the use of strategy if we don't have time to prepare? A good emergency hip-pocket strategy—one we carry with us for just this kind of situation—is this: get time to think. Just as it would have helped Jackie if she had set the conversation up in two parts, it would have helped Ross. If Jackie doesn't propose that strategy, Ross can. We tend to think of difficult conversations as single events, mostly because we just want to get them over with. But they don't have to be.

To get time to think, Ross doesn't have to pretend nothing is wrong. When her criticism takes him by surprise, he could say to Jackie, "I've worked with a lot of clients for a long time and reported to a lot of managers, and I've never heard anything like this. Your opinion of my attitude is very different from mine, and I don't think you've seen enough of my work to make a judgment. This performance review is important to me. But I have such a negative reaction to what you just said that I want to collect my thoughts and get back to you. Can we schedule another time to talk?"

Everything he says there is true to his sense of what's happening. At

him as they did for other people, and he wanted to polish his technique. He was satisfied, however, with the way he opened his negotiations. He told me he always began with the old chestnut "Those who can, do; those who can't, teach," and then would point out to the union that teachers work ten months of the year until three in the afternoon. He wanted to keep that opening and just buff up from there. Despite failing with it over and over again, disrespecting his counterparts was his preferred way of opening a conversation in which he intended to come to agree-the same time, he hasn't softened or escalated. Ross's approach here would be to step aside from a gut reaction, which isn't the same as not having one. He would speak briefly and clearly about the problem between Jackie and him. Then he would stop. If we're not in a crisis, only an extremely aggressive or frightened counterpart will decline to give us a chance to think. Jackie isn't in that category; most people aren't.

Breaking a difficult conversation in two is not the only way to work out strategy on your feet, of course. Ross could put preferred outcome as a question to Jackie—"Where are we trying to go here?" There will never be only one right thing to do.

It's worth noting, too, that this is not the first time Ross has heard unexpected bad news. It's not the first time for any of us. Difficult conversations happen; we have history with them. If we are often blindsided by difficult conversations, we might want to think about that. We might want to build some anticipatory strategy. We want the habit of good strategy for just those unexpected moments. We don't want to repeat and repeat ineffective approaches for a lifetime.

If they break the performance review in two, Jackie and Ross's follow-up conversation will still be difficult because the two of them are not headed in the same direction at this point. That hasn't changed. But the conversation will be a lot better—a lot less loaded and reactive—than the first one.

ment with them. Union officials loathed him and invested a lot of energy in thwarting him.

But the most pervasive reason that respect is rare and hard to put into play is rooted in the combat mind-set. Dominance and deference are opposite poles on the control spectrum in difficult conversation. People trying to get, or hang on to, the one-up dominance position are reluctant to show respect toward their counterpart, because they see it as a sign of weakness. Because zero-sum thinking is so closely tied to the combat mind-set, they also see respect as a limited commodity—there probably isn't enough to go around. They want to get respect and don't want to give it. But as always, their counterpart invariably resists playing along.

Are self-interest, self-protection, and self-respect enough incentive in the face of obstacles like these? Yes. Lack of respect is hard on reputations and relationships. It keeps difficult conversations out of balance and tilted toward failure.

In the revised version of her conversation with Ross, Jackie put respect into play by the *way* she set up the review. Ross put respect into play in his revised version, again in the *way* he stopped the conversation before it fell apart. We can begin to balance the conversation unilaterally, as they did. If we're in a conversation with someone who is escalating—as Jackie thought Ross was doing—we can say, "I don't know whether you're challenging me here or pushing back on the issue."

But while we do want to bring respect to a difficult conversation unilaterally, we don't want to bring it alone. Respect does not look weak or deferential if it is joined to self-respect.

## Self-respect

The self-respect that balances our respect toward our counterpart has nothing to do with a sense of superiority, self-righteousness, or entitlement. It's a more solid quality than those. At the same time, we know only too well that we can grant respect, grant respect, grant respect, over and over, and not get any back—and in difficult conversations, asking for mutual respect may not work. So we're going to bring our own self-respect, and because our counterpart isn't helping here, it has to be solid.

Self-respect doesn't *stand in* for strategy, the way self-righteousness sometimes does; self-respect is *part* of strategy. It's the part that lets us hold our own with our counterpart, but it's also the part that requires us to own what we do. It's Didion's kind of "moral nerve," the "habit of mind" brought to difficult conversation quite intentionally.[1] It's what keeps us out of conversational warfare, even when our counterpart is in full, self-righteous battle cry and we're outraged. In fact, many times our self-respect is standing right alongside our churning emotions. If we have moral nerve and have our eye on a good reputation and good relationships, our self-respecting habit of mind can't be stampeded by our feelings.

Just as we saw respect in Jackie's second version, we saw self-respect, too. She did not put herself down, weaken herself, or defer to Ross. We also saw self-respect in Ross's second version. He was surprised and angry, we know. But his self-respect showed the solidity that we're looking for. It kept him clear and balanced *at the same time* that he was surprised and angry. He couldn't manage that if he didn't have self-respect in balance with respect as a habit of mind. Finding balance between the two isn't going to occur to him, or us, in the moment.

### Respect the problem in the landscape

The third part of balanced respect in hard talks is respecting the problem in the landscape of the conversation. The problem between the two of us is not the same as the subject we're dealing with, although the subject is contributing to the problem—like the subject of Ross's attitude that set a match to his performance review with Jackie. But the problem in the conversation between them was more than Ross's attitude alone. It was the package deal: the topic, yes, but also the people involved, the stakes, the tough emotional reactions in play, and the ragged track of the conversation so far. *All* the pieces, together, constitute the problem in the landscape between them.

It is far more common to distort the problem or dismiss it, however, than respect the problem and plan strategy for it. Jackie, well-intentioned as she was, started off on that foot, misleading as it was, when she spoke dismissively about Ross's attitude as "one other thing I'd like to mention"—even though it was *the* significant problem to be faced. Tough personal feedback will always be hard to hear, and by minimizing it, Jackie practically set Ross up not to hear it at all. But when Ross did ignore the topic, Jackie was stumped, so she swapped her minimizing approach for "hit the point head on." The conversation deteriorated rapidly at that point, but not solely because the attitude issue was a sensitive one. In fact, the topic had barely been raised before it was snuffed out by distortion, belligerence, confusion, and accusations from both sides.

It takes time for the problems in the landscape to grow so big and put so much pressure on the people involved. But if strategy is a habit of mind and we acknowledge that tough conversations have problems that should not be distorted or dismissed, then we can start to plan how to deal with them. From their second efforts, we know that when Jackie and Ross had strategies that *assumed* there would be problems—even if Ross was taken by surprise and had to carve out time to strategize—the problems between the two of them didn't have time to grow so large. Respecting the problems in the landscape, including simply acknowledging that problems are there and calling them valid, helps balance a tough conversation, just as respect for our counterpart and self-respect do.

Three-way respect works like a zoom lens. It helps us respect the counterpart when that's helpful and zoom out and pan away to focus on the problem in the landscape, or on self-respect, when one of those will work better. It gives us a mobile kind of balance—it moves between the two players in the conversation and in and out of the conversational landscape, heading wherever imbalance threatens to get a foothold. Moving balance is a different game from the static tension between winning and losing, or between control and resistance to control. In fluid situations like tough conversations, we can't keep balance; we're constantly regaining balance, recovering from imbalance. We're never passive; we're creating balance moment to moment.

## Giving up the combat model

As we've seen repeatedly, the combat mind-set depends on imbalance in difficult conversations. The respect model works constantly to create and keep balance. That means the combat model and the respect model are fundamentally incompatible. If we try to layer three-way respect—respect toward our counterpart, self-respect, and respect for the problem between us—over the combat model, the dissonance between the two will drive us crazy. Trying to combine respect and warfare will bring out not just the tension and damage of power and control battles, but the dark twin of respect—manipulation or hypocrisy.

To find balance in difficult conversations, then, not only do we *want* to give up the combat mind-set, we *have* to give it up. That's bad news and good news. The bad news is that we can't give up the combat model a little bit. That will only work if our counterpart gives up on his side, too. And we can't control whether he will or not. Jackie tried giving up a little bit, but when Ross didn't reciprocate, she swung back hard.

The good news is that we can drop the combat model unilaterally. We can get ourselves out of the reactive, zero-sum, win-or-lose loop even if our counterpart stays in. We can be thinking not about beating people to the punch or getting what we want at their expense, but about where we're trying to go and who we want to be. We want strategy that works and that feels right and true when it works.

There is no clever trick to this, no magic bean. Strategy is the first step we take to get out of the combat model. Strategy gives us direction; it gets us halfway to where we want to be, but not all the way.

With so much emphasis here on strategy, and on respect as a working attitude, we are skirting something huge—difficult emotions themselves. Strategy is a thinking exercise. It doesn't have much to do with how we feel. In fact, by playing up strategy, we're probably trying to do better than how we feel. But what are we going to do about those tempestuous emotions?

# Remember:

- We need strategy for more than just our topic—we need strategy for how a tough conversation will play out—or we'll fall back into conversational warfare.

- Working out our *preferred outcome* gives us forward motion through expected and unexpected obstacles alike. Thinking it though keeps us realistic about what is possible.

- Working out our *preferred working relationship* and *interferences* with it keeps us strategically focused on the situation we have and the one we want—without blaming our problem on our counterpart or ourselves.

- A conversation with three-way respect as a strategy—respect for ourselves, our counterpart, and the problem between us—is in balance. It's hard to slide from there into zero-sum, personally adversarial warfare.

## CHAPTER 8

# Caught Up in Emotions

WE THINK difficult conversations are a power problem because, looked at one way, they are. But it's misleading to look at them as power problems alone, although many of us see them that way because, bad as that view is, to see them as emotional problems is worse. For most people in a difficult conversation, their worst nightmare is personality intertwined with issues. And when people think "personality," they mean bad behavior on the counterpart's side.

But that's not all. At the same time that we're dealing with their bad behavior, difficult conversations stir up crucially disturbing emotions on our own side—particularly fear, anger, and embarrassment.

Fear is the limiting emotion in difficult conversations. It is fear—and not some well-thought-out decision to pick our battles—that will keep us suffering in silence instead of going into a difficult conversation about a problem. If we do go into the conversation, fear makes it hard to think, as though our mind loses traction. And almost all of us want to hide our fear, which is hard to do when we're supposed to be talking.

Anger, on the other hand, can be a powerful motivation for taking up a problem and taking on a difficult conversation. But even more than fear, anger is hard on our reputation and our relationships, because anger usually looks and feels like unwarranted aggression to our counterparts. It might help us win in the short term, but hurt us badly over time.

Fear and anger are well-known primal emotions, but embarrassment is not usually seen as equally significant. Yet most people say that of the three, embarrassment—loss of face—is their biggest concern in difficult conversations. In fact, Kenneth Kendler, a psychiatric geneticist at Virginia Commonwealth University, considers that the need to maintain self-respect may be more central to the personality than is widely believed: "We are built to be status-protecting organisms."[1]

Taken one at a time, fear, anger, and embarrassment are easy to recognize. But they rarely come at us one at a time. When the conversation is tough, emotions feed into—and feed off—each other in inconsistent patterns, making it hard to see what we're dealing with at any point. Meanwhile, the fallout from emotions, whether they come separately or tangled together, is likely to be coming from both sides, simultaneously or alternately. So even though there are just three main problem emotions, and those three are familiar, they play out in the landscape of tough conversations in complicated ways. It's hard to come up with a general pattern of response that will consistently prevent the emotional fallout.

We saw this with Jane and Deirdre in chapter 6. Recall that Jane, the distribution coordinator, was berated by Deirdre, her angry boss, for not alerting Deirdre to an order screw-up that Jane had worked late into the night to correct. Jane was both embarrassed by the fallout from her part of the mistake and afraid of

Deirdre's anger. The coordinator kept apologizing, literally backing up, until Deirdre's tirade went on too long. At that point, and in her own defense, Jane snapped back angrily at Deirdre. In Jane's case, embarrassment and fear eventually fed into anger.

In that same conversation, when Jane finally snapped back at her, Deirdre too was embarrassed—at least momentarily—by her own lack of self-control. In Deirdre's case, however, fear never came into play. Finding herself embarrassed in front of her subordinate simply increased her anger. Deirdre's pattern is as recognizable as Jane's is, but we can't generalize from one pattern any more than we can from the other.

Even though we can't generalize about how emotions will play out in other people, individually we tend to run consistently along the same emotional tracks. Each of us has what I call a "signature emotional state" or two—an uncomfortable emotional mold we're caught in that's both hard to handle and hard to escape. And while no one likes his or her own fear, anger, or embarrassment, our signature emotional states offer us shreds of advantage. So at the same time that we want out of our emotional states, we also have reasons for sticking with them:

- For some of us, temperament and our history with difficult conversations make the way we handle them seem right to us. We always squelch our embarrassment with anger, say, or we always try to squelch our anger itself as long as we can, and negative reactions to our embarrassment or anger are just unavoidable fallout—the fault of the other person, really.

- For others—often those of us who pride ourselves on being rational in business—it's hard to admit to the emotional, irrational part of our own behavior at all when it crops up in a tough conversation. We stick with our signature emotional state simply because we can't identify it in ourselves well enough to handle it.

- For still others of us, the emotional reaction is the only part of a difficult conversation that feels genuine. The idea of "handling" our emotions seems intolerably manipulative, even when our signature state is painful or destructive.

- Finally, like lab rats in a stressful situation, some of us find it easier to stick with the distress we know than risk something new.

But these reasons for sticking with our signature emotional states are very, very small comfort in the face of huge and hurtful emotions. We want to, and we can, find ways to work this out better, both within ourselves and between us and our counterparts. To begin, let's look at three people who get tangled by emotion in a difficult conversation that has a particularly excruciating twist— it's a conversation that goes wrong in front of spectators.

## The college campaign meeting contretemps

Erica, director of special gifts at a New England college, was a highly successful development officer. Her success was largely due to the skill she brought to cultivating good and long-lasting donor relations and the creativity she brought to meeting donors' hopes and desires for their gifts while also meeting the college's needs. Erica was warm and funny—both donors and her staff were devoted to her. And she was deeply diplomatic.

Erica had scheduled an informational meeting with staff to discuss the next stage of the college's capital campaign. But some of the most important volunteers for this new stage of the campaign— who were not only alumni but also the college's biggest donors themselves—were coming to campus that week for homecoming. So Erica's boss, Stewart, the college's senior director of leadership giving, had asked Erica to change her plans. Stewart proposed instead that he would lead a larger meeting that would include not only Erica and her fund-raising staff, but also the volunteers on campus for homecoming, as well as Stewart's boss, Gordon, vice president of development at the college. Stewart had asked Erica to brief him on the informational component for this revised meeting, and she had done so.

Stewart was sure-footed with the broad vision of the capital campaign and was often in the limelight. But he sometimes took a little specific knowledge and ran with it. He did that now, when the conversation turned to details of the volunteers' fund-raising. Stewart told the group that an important focus of the next stage of the campaign would be to "go back to the well," soliciting again from corporations that had made previous donations. In fact, Stewart was mistaken. That was not the plan, and going back to the well had not been part of Erica's informational briefing. In response to Stewart's comment, there was some confusion, and Wilson, one of the prominent donor-volunteers, raised a question about the approach Stewart had just described. "No problem there," Stewart confidently told everyone. "We've seen this approach work before—we'll get more money for less work by sticking with corporate donations."

Erica cringed when she heard Stewart's reply. She couldn't leave the volunteers with such a big misunderstanding about the actual fund-raising plan. Still, she hesitated to speak. Why?

There's some history here. Stewart, Erica's boss, was very good at the strategic parts of his job, but he had been steadily promoted through managerial positions more for his strategic vision than for his management expertise. In fact, the management of staff was both stressful and mysterious to him. Partly to keep his staff at bay, Stewart took what he considered a "tough but fair" stance with them. An administrator at his level said of Stewart, "I wouldn't call him tough, but he is a bit rigid when he might be wrong." In contrast to that, a former staff member who had left Stewart's department heard the "tough but fair" comment and laughed. He said, "Stewart is an emotional bully to anyone below him. Part of his bullying is to speak abusively to people who work for him and then require that we agree with him. That's where he gets the 'fair' part—you have to agree that he's right. The people in his department live in terror for their jobs."

Erica was caught in that bind. In the past, if she had corrected mistaken information when Stewart spoke, even in meetings with much smaller stakes than this, Stewart would later claim that she had intentionally tried to show him up and he would really retaliate. But if she said nothing at the time, and he found out about an error later, he would be angry and accusatory about that, too. In this meeting with the volunteers, even though she was completely familiar with the details of the campaign plan, Erica simply didn't know whether to say anything about Stewart's incorrect information.

Finally, Erica decided to take the risk—Stewart's comment was too far off the mark to leave in the air. Because fund-raising professionals like Erica are nothing if not tactful, she believed that by giving Stewart as much cover as she could, she would give him a chance to move on smoothly. And so she spoke up.

"In the larger sense, you're absolutely right, Stewart," Erica said. "That has been and still is one of the college's most successful strategies. This stage of the campaign is focused on funds for buildings, however, and the corporate gifts tend to be restricted to supporting particular faculty research initiatives. We do always want to keep the money-to-work ratio as high as we can, as you put it so well. But just for this phase, we're going to ask our volunteers to shift focus a bit and use their personal networks to raise individual donations for name-worthy buildings."

When Erica finished speaking, Stewart looked first at his boss, Gordon, then at the volunteers, and finally at Erica herself. He did have some recollection of her point from their briefing. Nevertheless, after a moment, he smiled at her and said, "No, Erica, you have your information wrong. You've been beavering away at your level, and you're not privy to the big picture. It's not your fault that Gordon and I get more information in the locker room than you do in the powder room, is it?" Erica looked at Stewart in silence and then looked at the floor.

Here Stewart wagged his finger at Erica and said joshingly, "But I'm not sure you have a handle on the job. I may have to fire you if you can't keep up." Turning to the others in the room, he said, "I had a secretary who couldn't keep up, and I had to fire her." To make sure people knew he was joking, he went on with a wink and a chuckle, "Too bad, because she was cute. And available."

Gordon, Stewart's boss, was not laughing, however. No one was. In the silence that followed Stewart's last remarks, Gordon shifted uneasily in his chair. Then he stood, rubbed his hands briskly together, and—instead of speaking to the conspicuous shambles before him—proposed that they all break for lunch. "Let's see if we can reconcile these different points of view and pick up our game plan this afternoon," he said. As people were leaving the room, one of the senior donors walked up to Erica, extended his hand, and asked if she would join his table.

When all the others except the two of them had left the room, Gordon turned to Stewart and said, "I think you've crossed a line on a couple of fronts, Stewart. We have policies at this school, and I don't want all of HR breathing down my neck. If we want to avoid any firings here, you owe Erica an apology, and you'd better do it today."

Stewart replied, "I was kidding! Erica knew that; they all knew it. It was obvious—I'm a married man!"

Gordon said, "I know that, Stewart. I'm not sure that makes it better. You think about your apology. Too many people heard you in there, and they were the wrong people."

After that, Stewart chased down the corridor after Erica and caught her alone. He said, "That wasn't so bad, was it?" he asked. "I didn't mean anything by it. You shouldn't contradict me in front of others."

## What happened here?

This conversation has gone wrong for everyone: for Erica and Stewart, certainly, but for Gordon, the vice president, too. Two parts of the problem are familiar from chapter 6. First, there are power issues in the picture, with bosses and subordinates on more than one level: Erica works for Stewart, both of them work for Gordon, and they all work for the donors. Second, Stewart, at least, had a combat mentality in his skirmish with Erica: from his point of view, they were in a zero-sum conversation that would have just one winner and one loser.

Power issues did turn up the heat. But simply put, it was not a power battle that pushed the conversation over the edge for Stewart or Erica. It was the fallout from their signature combinations of emotions.

If we want to find ways to get ourselves out of these difficult conversations intact or to keep out of them in the first place, we certainly won't get far, as we saw in chapter 6, by trying to shoehorn all tough conversations into the "one-up wins, one-down loses" cliché. But we've also seen before that trying to put conversations back on track by reducing the question to who was right and who was wrong won't shed much light on how to improve them, either. It's easy to see Stewart as the bad guy here, a bully and a buffoon. It's always easy to see a difficult conversation as one with a bad guy and a victim. Reversing the roles, Stewart certainly thought Erica herself was a bad actor at the time. And it looked as though Gordon, the most senior manager there, just punted, hoping that a little time and distance would lessen the effects of a calamity he didn't cause and didn't want to claim. It's a little more complicated to see that each of them—Erica, Stewart, and Gordon—was caught up in an emotional morass of his or her own. Nevertheless, it's more useful to look into those tangles than to act like the Three Stooges, pointing fingers at anyone but themselves.

Let's pull this example apart enough to see what happened and what can be done about it. We'll look first at Stewart because, from everyone's point of view except his, the conversation's downward slide started with him.

### Stewart

Stewart found himself in what seemed to him to be a power-challenge conversation with Erica—but made worse for him by being played out in front of other people. As with so many situations that make us both embarrassed and angry, to some degree he brought this on himself. Stewart had stepped in to lead an important meeting after only lightweight preparation. More to the point, it's likely that this is not the first time he's been overconfident, underprepared, and embarrassed.

But in this meeting, Stewart had an excellent backup source of information—Erica. Instead of using her as an ally when he was questioned by Wilson, however, he saw her as a competitor. This takes us back to the zero-sum perspective so characteristic when a challenge to power appears to be under way: Stewart acted as though there were not enough expert prestige to go around. From that point of view, Stewart would lose some prestige if any went to Erica. He would not willingly be a party to a bad deal like that. So at the same time that he had a habit of getting into deep water, Stewart pushed himself away from a nearby lifesaving ring.

Two things then happened. First, Stewart realized he had made a mistake in his information. Second, he wasn't easily able to correct it. He didn't have good enough technique to get himself out of what he'd gotten himself into. So he did what many of us do when we can't see how to make a difficult conversation go better— he got angry and made it worse. He retaliated against Erica, because he saw her as the cause of his embarrassment, and he used humor as a fig leaf to cover both his embarrassment and his anger. Those two weren't Stewart's only emotional troubles: moments later, when Gordon talked to him alone, fear for his own job was added to Stewart's embarrassment and anger.

Stewart was tangled in his signature emotional state—the uncomfortable emotional mess he found hard to manage or to escape. His anger fed off his embarrassment, and then, by his reaction to those two emotions, he found himself staring down the barrel of fear.

### Erica

Erica's signature emotional state was less straightforward. Because she had worked for Stewart for some time, she had seen his bullying pattern before. Privately, she called it "Set himself up, fall on his face, blame someone else, and make that one pay." But Erica did not see her own pattern as clearly in the "You're attacking me!" conversation she found herself in.

Under Stewart's attack and his not-funny-at-all threat, Erica understandably suffered embarrassment and fear, but not the fear we might expect at first glance. Yes, she had been apprehensive about correcting Stewart. But when he did attack, her main fear was that she would embarrass herself by overreacting to him. Why? Because Erica was also angry. She was angry with herself that she had initially hesitated to speak up—she thought she should have been bolder—and she was angry with Stewart for turning on her and embarrassing her when she had so carefully avoided doing that to him.

For Erica, however, the difficult conversation and her more complicated signature emotional state began before Stewart attacked her. When she first overcame her hesitation and plunged in, Erica followed a tack that I call *hypernice*, a term for exaggerated niceness and appeasement. Hypernice is tact gone over the top. People act hypernice when they are working hard to avoid even the faintest suggestion of aggression. In Erica's case, she was trying to cover for Stewart at the same time that she corrected his factual error. Familiar with Stewart's emotional bullying, Erica feared that she would offend him and worked hard not to. Internally, she had to juggle both her uneasy emotions and her effort to be nice enough to manage the tricky moment.

But as we saw, even hypernice didn't work. Erica saw that, too, of course, but she had a more complicated emotional response to her unsuccessful moment than Stewart had to his. Yes, she was angry with Stewart for humiliating her. But she was also still angry with herself. Part of Erica believed that her failure to appease Stewart—at the same time that she corrected what he said— was her own fault. If only she had been even nicer, even more placating, she could have done better.

So while Stewart was lashing out at Erica in front of the others, Erica herself was tied up in knots. She was angry, but she was also afraid: she was understandably afraid that anything she said at that point, however hypernice and appeasing, would kindle another attack. But she was also afraid that if she spoke at all, her pent-up anger would burst out and would look like an immense overreaction. Horrible as it was to be embarrassed by Stewart, it would have been worse for her to embarrass herself. As a result, the anger and fear in her signature emotional state were as much directed against herself as they were against her counterpart, Stewart.

### Gordon

Stewart and Erica were not the only people in this conversation with a problem. Gordon, senior to both Stewart and Erica, couldn't simply sit there with his hands folded, watching the meltdown in front of him. After Stewart's wayward jokes, Gordon spoke because he realized that the whole roomful of people, not just Erica, had a problem with Stewart's demeaning remarks. Gordon had to deal with the situation in the room, and he also had to deal with his own signature emotional state.

He was angry to find himself in such a position—needing to deal publicly with a mess made by two subordinates. He was also embarrassed, certain that the confrontation reflected badly on his shop and, by extension, badly on him.

Perhaps worst of all, Gordon was afraid of mishandling the situation. To begin with, he was an administrator with a strong rational suit and an aversion to squishiness. He found it awkward to step in and handle the emotional debacle between Stewart and Erica, particularly in front of spectators. At the same time, the question of how he ought to handle the situation looked very delicate to him, with lots of room for mistakes and not much chance of getting it right. The odds of success didn't look good, and Gordon didn't take them. Instead of handling the situation, he entirely sidestepped it by breaking for lunch. For Gordon, this was an "I can't go there" conversation, and his particular combination of anger, embarrassment, and fear shut down his ability to act in the moment at all.

### Different emotional combinations, shared roots

Emotion had gotten the upper hand with everyone in the contretemps between Erica and Stewart, and emotion was directing the course of this conversation a lot more than power was. From the outside, we can see that there are about as many ways that big emotions combine into signature states as there are people in a difficult conversation. But the different combinations do share three common roots.

First, emotional history gets replayed. Stewart has retaliated before when he thought he was losing face, and Erica has turned anger against herself and fallen silent before, too. In this conversation, neither retaliation nor silence was particularly successful, but a move doesn't have to work well to become a habit. (Anyone who says "um" a lot knows that.)

Second, there's a common viruslike lock between a thwarting ploy on one side and vulnerability to the ploy on the other, even though the lock can be hard to see at first. For example, Stewart was vulnerable to Gordon's warning about Stewart's own job, while Erica was vulnerable to Stewart's poisonous joke. Not everyone is equally vulnerable to a given ploy. In this case, Stewart and Erica reacted instantly, albeit differently, to those two ploys *because* they were vulnerable to the ploys, not because of the choice of ploys themselves.

Third, for almost everyone, the combination of ploy plus emotional vulnerability sets up more than a reaction; it very frequently sets up an overreaction. And every emotional overreaction sends us further and further out of balance. We saw, for example, that the more Stewart's humor was shunned, the further he pushed the joke. And we also saw that when Stewart dismissed

Erica's careful comment and belittled her, she shut herself down into complete silence.

Is there anything we can do to break the grip of such strong and ingrained emotional history, habit, and reaction? David Mamet would say yes. The Pulitzer Prize–winning playwright works with actors—people whose job requires them to perform well even while their emotions are strongly stirred. Mamet gives clear and practical advice about how to make it work:

> *Your feelings are not within your control . . . acting, like carpentry, is a craft with a definite set of skills and tools. By assiduously applying your will to the acquiring of those skills and tools, you will eventually make them habitual. Once your skills become habitual, you need no longer concentrate on your technique . . . Remember, you do not have to feel like performing your action. If you learn to act in spite of what you are feeling, you will bring yourself to life in the scene . . .*
>
> *Once you've learned to commit fully to a physical action, your only task concerning emotions will be to learn to work through them, to let them exist as they will, for they are beyond your control . . . you will learn to work through the torrents of emotion . . . your one and only job is to follow through.*[2]

If we substitute "hard talks" for "physical action," then Mamet has put his finger on what we need to do to handle ourselves well at the same time that our big emotions are strongly in play. We too have to learn to get through a difficult conversation skillfully, "in spite of what we are feeling." But how?

## Remember:

- The big three problem emotions we get caught up in—fear, anger, and embarrassment—combine differently into individual signature emotional states.

- Our signature emotional states replay our emotional history, almost never helpfully.

- We can break the grip of our signature emotional states by handling a tough conversation skillfully— at the same time our big three emotions are in play.

## CHAPTER 9

# Out of Emotion's Grip

## *Increasing Skill*

A LOT OF WHAT'S DIFFICULT in toxic conversations has emotional roots, but not emotional solutions. Yes, we have our signature emotional states, with anger, embarrassment, or fear thrown in. And to be sure, it's unrealistic to ask people to stop having the feelings they have. So rather than ask for the improbable, we will accept that there are strong emotions in difficult conversations—but we won't stop there. As David Mamet says, handling ourselves well isn't based on how we feel.

We need to add real skill to prevent our emotions from jamming us up. Only after our skill increases and our outcomes get better will the grip of big emotions loosen. To get real skill, we need to give up two familiar approaches. First, we cannot keep trying to throttle our emotions with the control model—insisting that we *must* control our emotions. And second, we don't want to run in the opposite direction, overreacting willy-nilly to whatever comes up in the conversation—insisting that we *can't* control our emotions.

If we take away both emotional control and emotional over-reaction, we need good, functional tactics to put in their place:

- **FIND THE MIDDLE GROUND BETWEEN EMOTIONAL EXTREMES.** The choice between choking off our feelings and letting them rip is itself an extreme choice. When we find a balance point between emotional extremes, we can choose what to do or which way to move from that mid-point, not from the outermost emotional poles.

- **IMMUNIZE OURSELVES AGAINST THWARTING PLOYS.** We stop simply reacting to what's thrown at us and learn to protect ourselves where we're vulnerable. This is like scientists who, when studying how a pathogen compromises a cell, focus on the cell, not the bug—but we'll focus on ourselves.

- **CHANGE TACK.** When a conversation is going south, most of us have such a small stock of tactics to use that when the first thing we try doesn't work, we just keep on doing it. We need more ways to handle the rough patches. It's more effective and much easier when we have several tacks we can take.

- **RECOVER FROM MISTAKES.** Even with the best will in the world, we'll still make mistakes. Given that, we need a sound technique for recovering from them, so that a blunder doesn't take on a life of its own and move to center stage in the conversation.

We will highlight each of these four tactics separately, but we'll also see that there is movement back and forth among them. Thwarting ploys don't come one at a time, and we often weave good countering tactics together to meet and offset them.

Looking back at the campaign meeting, it's clear that Erica and Stewart's conversation had gone completely out of balance by the time it was over. But there's no question that these four basic tactics—finding middle ground, protecting ourselves against thwarting ploys, changing tack, and recovering from error—could have snatched the conversation from the jaws of defeat.


# First tactic: Find middle ground

We saw that Erica did not succeed in avoiding damage to herself— or to Stewart—during the campaign meeting. Odd as it sounds, she may have tried too hard. Because she didn't want to give offense, Erica wasn't simply nice when she spoke up; she was hypernice. In practice, however, *hypernice* and *offensive* are far apart from one another; in fact, they're polar opposites. But as so often happens in a confrontation, Erica could see no middle ground between the two. In her eyes, *hypernice* and *offensive* were right up against one another—if she weren't careful to be extra nice, she would slip over into offensiveness. But *hypernice* didn't save Erica, and with *offensive* out of bounds, she found herself with nowhere to go.

It's common to hear people, like Erica, say that extreme choices are all they have in difficult situations. A politician's wife accosted by an angry constituent in the supermarket said, "What could I do? Shout back? I had no choice but to ditch my cart and leave the store." Taking the opposite perspective, a new school administrator told an older, surprised colleague, "I had to be as harsh as I was with the office staff so they wouldn't think I was a pushover." The problem isn't that those are two wrong ways to handle their respective situations, although the tactics do give one pause. The problem is that both the politician's wife and the school administrator, like Erica, believed their choices were so limited and so polar.

Even if we're used to seeing polar opposites like offensive/ hypernice or shout/silence or harsh/pushover as right up against each other, there is another, better way to look at them. Think of a folding fan—when it's closed, the two ends are all we see; when we open it up, there's a lot more inside. As a matter of fact, a wide range of responses always exists between the extreme ends in any conversation. What does the range of responses between two extremes look like, and how would we find the midpoint? (See figure 9-1.)

### Range of response

Shelly's predicament shows the whole range of possible responses. This level-headed financial manager of a chain of casual-dining restaurants was in a meeting with seven other managers when one of them, Kim, told a racist joke. It offended Shelly, who was rarely caught off guard. Shelly wasn't sure how to respond. Let's look at her options—we'll work our range-of-response model from each end.

- **PLAY ALONG.** This is the most passive response possible, more passive than doing nothing. If Shelly, who was offended

FIGURE 9-1

**Range of response to thwarting ploys**

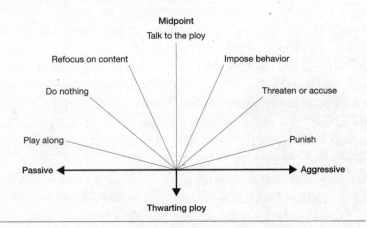

by Kim's joke, had laughed along, Shelly would have gone to the farthest passive end of the range of responses.

- **DO NOTHING.** This is where people like Shelly start if they are surprised by a thwarting ploy and uncertain what to do. (Is a joke a thwarting ploy? It may be. A thwarting ploy and a vulnerability are a package deal. If Shelly is vulnerable to an offensive joke, it's a thwarting ploy for her. Is it intentional? We don't know—and we need a way to respond, whether we can or can't read intentions accurately.) The *do nothing* response is hard to read. Shelly may lead Kim to believe that the joke was perfectly acceptable, even a success. Or, if Kim were acting maliciously, no response from Shelly (*do nothing*) could be read as capitulation.

- **PUNISH.** If we swing all the way to the other extreme of our range, to the opposite of passivity, the most aggressive response to a ploy is punishment. If Shelly had stood up, reached across the table, and slapped Kim (as she might have done if this had been a movie), that would be punishment for the joke. But punishment can come in many forms and can vary widely in its severity. It would also be punishment if Shelly hired a lawyer and sued Kim or the company. It might or might not have been punishment if Shelly had walked out of the meeting. *Punish* is a bigger category than *do nothing*.

- **THREATEN OR ACCUSE.** This isn't as punitive as a lawsuit, but it's well along in the aggressive range. Shelly could accuse Kim, saying, "You are such a racist," or could threaten, "If you ever tell a joke like that again, I'll see that you don't work here anymore." There are many shades of response between the points picked out here. If Shelly had confronted Kim with a senior HR manager at her side, that action would split the difference between *threaten* and *punish* in the range of responses.

- **REFOCUS ON CONTENT.**  This response returns to the topic of discussion that preceded the thwarting ploy. After Kim's joke, Shelly might have left a significant pause and then said, "Let's go back to the numbers." She might have used a tone of voice or body language that suggested, "I'm not going to respond to that." Returning to the topic is closer to middle ground than is playing along or doing nothing at all. But it's still more passive than midpoint on our model. Why isn't Shelly at midpoint if she refocuses on the numbers? What's passive about that? By only hinting at her disapproval of the joke, Shelly isn't talking to Kim's ploy itself. Shelly is using an indirect response that has to be interpreted and accepted if it is going to work. If Shelly's remark is misinterpreted, or ignored, or isn't interpreted at all, Kim is off the hook.

- **IMPOSE BEHAVIOR.**  With this response, we're telling the counterpart what to do or what not to do. "You shouldn't tell that kind of joke" tells Kim what not to do. "You might want to save that for after five o'clock" tells Kim what to do. This is the way parents often talk to children, which may have something to do with why it isn't quite neutral in a conversation between adults.

All these options—and all the shadings in between—are genuine choices in response to a thwarting ploy. We all use some of them or have had them used on us, so we recognize them. The less passive and less aggressive ploys are not only familiar but also comfortable to those who use them. But they don't strike the midpoint. How do we find true midpoint, the neutral ground between passive and aggressive in this range of responses?

- **TALK TO THE PLOY.**  If Shelly says, "A joke like that doesn't work for me," she is speaking to the ploy her counterpart has just used. She needs to speak *clearly* enough that Kim knows what the problem was; she needs to speak *neutrally*—without intonation or body language that exaggerates or mixes the message; and she needs to speak with *temperate* phrasing that isn't easy to reject. There is no single phrase that's specifically necessary. Shelly could also say, "When a joke is funny to you but isn't to me, I don't know what to say"—she'll find her own words—and she would still be on middle ground.

### Finding middle ground: The tactic in play

How would finding middle ground play out with Erica, Stewart, and Gordon in the campaign meeting? Let's look first at Erica. If she had gone to the midpoint on the range of response and chosen *talk to the ploy*, how would it sound in practice?

Remember that Stewart had ended, jokingly, with "I'm not sure you have a handle on the job. I may have to fire you if you can't keep up. I had a secretary who couldn't keep up, and I had to fire her. Too bad, because she was cute. And available."

If in the silence that followed, Erica wanted to go to the midpoint between an aggressive response (offensive) and a passive one (hypernice), she would "talk to the ploy," by saying, "Let's talk about women who work for you, and who make mistakes, another time." She might go on to say, "It may be that we have an honest disagreement here about the current fund-raising approach, or it may be that we have a misunderstanding. Let's hold that aside for now, and I'll check on it. If I've made a mistake, I'll apologize to you all."

Does that sound too harsh? Shouldn't Erica have saved face for her boss if she could? That's an option. But is it the right division of labor? Should the target of an attack mop up afterward? If in this new version, Erica didn't speak gently enough for you, your own familiar feel for the midpoint might be west of center, toward the passive end of the span. But when you have something difficult to say, will you either soften it beyond recognition or say nothing? In the original conversation, Erica's midpoint was off-center, and she said nothing at all.

Does the midpoint response sound too soft? Aren't some things, including Stewart's humiliating joke, simply out of bounds? Shouldn't Erica have confronted him? That's an option. In fact, Stewart himself chose it. He *meant* his remarks and the joke to be confrontational: he thought Erica was out of bounds in the first place for contradicting him in front of others. If your feel for the midpoint is east of center—at least when you're angry and embarrassed and think the counterpart should get what she deserves—will you cause the same damage to your own reputation and relationships that Stewart caused to his?

When we're in a tight situation, the midpoint gives us a good place to go *to*. We are always likely to shut down, do again what hasn't worked before, or react to our counterpart when we don't know where we're going. The midpoint is a positive place to put our minds, letting us focus on how to go forward in the conversation and do it in a way that isn't passive, aggressive, or a wild swing between the two.

The midpoint is full of benefits. We can speak from there to a counterpart who is one-up, one-down, or parallel to us—alone or in front of others. Our emotional state may still be in force, but the way we're handling ourselves is balanced. Our counterpart may still throw stuff at us—thwarting ploys rarely come one at a time—but we don't lose self-respect or drop respect for our counterpart, because it's the ploy itself that we speak to. Working from the midpoint is the difference between hitting the tennis ball coming at us and, at one extreme, throwing down our racket or, at the other extreme, flinging it at our counterpart's head.

We've seen this work well before. In chapter 4, David spoke from the midpoint when Rachel didn't credit his academic report: "Rachel, you'll want to credit those findings to my research with Professor Sullivan." And in chapter 7, Ross spoke from the midpoint when Jackie took him by surprise with criticism during his performance review: "Your opinion of my attitude is very different from mine, and I don't think you've seen enough of my work to make a judgment." Both David and Ross were having strong emotional reactions at the time. But their responses, like Erica's reimagined version of her response, came from the midpoint. (If those responses look soft or harsh, check whether your feel for the midpoint, especially when you yourself are having a strong emotional reaction, lies east or west of the middle on the span of responses.)

Finding the midpoint when we're caught up in our own emotions is an acquired skill. In regular conversation, we speak from the midpoint most of the time, and all we need to do is bring this skill from the calm to the storm. Of course, there's the rub. Our confidence that we can find the midpoint at all will often fade in the face of thwarting ploys. Why do people use them? How do thwarting ploys get under our skin? And what can we do about them?

## Second tactic: Immunize against thwarting ploys

There is a nonvenomous snake in Massachusetts called the hognose snake. It just eats toads. But when it's alarmed, the hognose snake inflates its body, hisses loudly, lunges forward, and spreads a cobralike hood. If that doesn't work to scare off whatever has alarmed it, the hognose writhes, vomits, and then rolls over on its back and lets its tongue hang out like a dead snake. If you turn it over, it will immediately roll on its back again, because it's "dead."

The hognose snake is an expert at thwarting ploys.

Many of us have a hard time with a counterpart who refuses to reason, who lies, who threatens, who stonewalls, who cries, or who acts insulted and defensive. Those are thwarting ploys. The hardest part of a difficult conversation is usually not the subject or the counterpart, but the counterpart's ploys—at least those we're hot-wired to react to. Counterparts don't shout, lie, threaten, or refuse to reason because they are crazy or vicious. Instead, like the hognose snake, they are trying to stop a threat. Even if we pose the threat at the moment, thwarting ploys are not exactly aimed at us personally. Thwarting ploys are strong, fixed patterns. Counterparts use them out of habit, sometimes even unconsciously, or because they have had success with them in the past. Whatever the counterpart's motive for using a thwarting ploy—clumsiness, fear, malice—there is a great deal we can do about the ploy on our own side.

Just as a pathogen needs to latch onto a cell's vulnerable point to damage it, so too does a thwarting ploy need our vulnerability to trigger a reaction from us. If we're not vulnerable, the ploy will roll off and we don't have to think about it. If we are vulnerable, we have three choices: react again and again, make our counterpart stop using the ploy, or immunize ourselves. Immunizing ourselves is our best bet.

The good news about our vulnerabilities to thwarting ploys is that we know what our vulnerabilities are. We tend to be susceptible to the same ploys for decades. If we are not provoked by someone shouting at us, shouting has probably rolled off us for a long time; if we *are* provoked by shouting, this is probably not the first time. Just as habit drives most thwarting ploys, habit drives our reactions to them. Why is that good news?

Knowing our vulnerabilities is good news because we can begin to build skill around them in moments of calm, instead of reacting to them when our nerves are on edge as a conversation starts to go badly. We can't predict when a ploy will be thrown at us, but we can determine how we'll handle ourselves when it is. Knowing our vulnerabilities is good news because we can break the viral lock of ploy and vulnerability unilaterally, instead of hoping our counterpart will change. Don't ever count on the other person to change in a tough conversation. And it's good news because we can stop being afraid of our own reactions, including fear of the damage those reactions will do. Fear that advises us to pick our battles with care makes sense. But fear of thwarting ploys and our reactions to them is awfully limiting. It's like being afraid we'll get wet in the rain. Of course we're going to get wet: the question is, have we brought an umbrella? Let's see how some-one vulnerable to a thwarting ploy decided to immunize herself and break out of the ploy-reaction pattern unilaterally.

Kate, a young senior manager in a museum, worked with sophisticated but volatile colleagues. The museum was undertak-ing a major renovation, which is a lengthy and delicate business when you're working around priceless art and a community of people. In a planning meeting, one of Kate's colleagues, Eliza-beth, finally proposed that the museum simply close a wing that provided entry to a classroom from the surrounding galleries.

"We'll close down the wing, and people will have to deal with it," she said. "They just won't have access through there."

"We can do that, but we need to be careful," Kate replied. "If classes are in session, students need to get through there. It will affect both schedules and other space if they can't."

Elizabeth dismissed the objection: "Now, Kate, you're getting overemotional."

Kate was startled into silence as she replayed her own comment, unable to see anything overemotional in what she had said or in how she had said it. Still, she thought, maybe it was true. The con-versation went on while she half-pondered and half-listened. Then, to make matters worse, a few minutes later, Jeffrey, another man-ager, made the same objection to Elizabeth's point that Kate had made earlier. This time, the others accepted it without remarks about Jeffrey's emotions.

"That's enough," Kate thought to herself.

This was not the first time Elizabeth had chided her for being overemotional; nor was it the first time Kate had reacted to the remark—she knew she was vulnerable to that thwarting ploy. The allegation was a particularly devilish ploy because it made Kate look girlish and unprofessional in a group of polished man-agers. And so, understandably, Kate consistently had a strong, embarrassed reaction to it. At the same time, she knew it was an easy ploy for Elizabeth to choose if Elizabeth wanted to get a rise out of her. And, of course, getting a rise out of Kate would confirm the allegation. Because the ploy worked to make her either react or fall silent, Kate realized that she was basically teaching Elizabeth to use the very ploy to which she, Kate, was vulnerable if Elizabeth wanted to dismiss Kate's objections or silence Kate altogether.

Kate had had enough of that. She didn't want to go through any more meetings waiting for the predictable trigger and worrying about her reaction. She had three choices: hope it never happened again, blame Elizabeth for using the ploy and suffer through it, or immunize herself.

Kate chose to immunize. To use the new tactic, she had conditions she had to satisfy. She couldn't attack or back down—she needed to neutralize the ploy. And she had to find something she could say in front of other people. Finally, of course, she had to be able to handle the ploy even when she had a strong, embarrassed reaction to it. It was a tall order, but she was game.

Kate took a lesson from the range of response diagram in figure 9-1 and decided to go straight to midpoint. She would talk to the ploy. Playing a little on being the youngest in the group, she came up with a question for Elizabeth: "Show me how you would make my point without sounding overemotional." It met all three conditions—she neutralized the ploy, found something she could say in front of others, and withstood her own embarrassment at being called overemotional. Satisfied, Kate put it in her hip pocket, ready to use when the ploy showed up again.

With that response at hand, Kate felt completely different. She said to me, "Now I almost hope it comes up again. I've spent a lot of time caught up in dread and embarrassment, but now what I feel is . . . ready. In fact, now I want to think up some other good responses to the 'overemotional' ploy, just for the luxury of choosing what I'll do."

Kate was immunizing herself against her own vulnerability to a particular ploy. Specifically, she meant to neutralize the ploy itself. What surprised her, however, was that she had also defused her own emotional reaction. She felt much more balanced, not likely to swing from an embarrassed silence to an embarrassed reaction. Even though she anticipated having to respond to Elizabeth while in the grip of embarrassment, her emotional reaction itself cooled down almost completely once Kate felt more competent to handle the conversation.

In fact, Elizabeth's ploy did show up again, but Kate didn't use her first hip-pocket phrase. By then, she had worked up a whole pack of them, all with the same neutral, disarming characteristics. And so as soon as she raised a new point of view and heard "overemotional," Kate smiled and said, "I kind of like this picture of me as wild and windblown, but what I really am is the loyal opposition." Elizabeth was surprised and quiet for a moment. Then she said, "I know you are."

With practice, we will eventually be able to immunize in the moment, while we are right in the middle of a hard talk. But at first, we'll probably have to work it out during calmer moments. Remember that conversation is not combat—don't retaliate and don't surrender. Go to the midpoint between those extremes, and work toward disarming the ploy itself.

## Third tactic: Change tack

We now know that self-immunizing will put us in better balance while we're caught in our own emotional heavy weather. But that wouldn't have been enough to get Stewart out of his predicament in the campaign meeting. He was caught up in tough emotions himself, but what he *did* was even worse than how he *felt*.

When Stewart caught up with Erica after the meeting, he told her, "That wasn't so bad, was it? I didn't mean anything by it." Whether or not he did mean anything by his remarks, how did Stewart get so far out on such a dangerous limb without intending to?

Two things came together to get him there. First, Stewart thought Erica's correction made him lose face in front of the donors. So, consistent with his "tough but fair" style, he would be tough by cracking down on Erica for her insubordination, and he would be fair by evening the score: if she embarrassed him, then he would embarrass her back.

Second, Stewart not only had a two-part battle plan, but also had a two-part ploy in mind, one that should work out for him even in front of an audience: he would use the iron fist in the velvet glove. He would put Erica in her place, but he would use humor to do it. This is, in its way, an effort to be fair and balanced—Stewart would not come down too hard, yet he would not be too soft. However, the plan was not only complicated to orchestrate, it was tricky to control. Stewart would have to cover up his own embarrassment and at the same time make sure Erica took in his anger. The others would have to see neither anger nor embarrassment, but humor alone.

That's hard to pull off, but it is characteristic of people who use the combat model to have firmly in mind a scenario for how ploys will work. They often imagine in considerable detail how the scene will play out, what they will say, and how others will react to them. Caught up in their own scripts, they stick with a ploy even when in real time it isn't working well at all. And so Stewart didn't rethink his ploy when his first gibe at Erica failed to get a laugh. He kept at it, in fact laying it on even thicker. What began as a dig meant to put Erica in her place degenerated into a coarse putdown and a bald threat. By the end, Stewart paid a high price—a threat to his own job—but he could no more give up his ploy than he could give up his idea of how it should have been received. Why not? Because he had nothing to put in its place.

Instead of locking into a scenario he created himself, Stewart needed to change tacks. His problem was not that "tough but fair" is the wrong approach in difficult conversation, although the way Stewart used it here is hard to recommend. His problem was that he needed a better answer to the question "What will I do if it doesn't work?" than "Do it more." We can't count on a scenario that depends on a certain response from the other side. A plotted scenario might work if people's patterns of reaction were consistently the same, but they are not. Stewart would put himself in a much stronger position to move off a tack that isn't taking him where he wants to go if he immunized first.

Stewart blamed Erica for his anger and embarrassment, but those emotions were his own. If Stewart assessed what triggered him the most in difficult conversations—if he checked out his own vulnerabilities—he would certainly come up with "losing face" as one of them (although he might call it something else). How can we be sure? Think back to when Stewart caught up with Erica in the hallway. He quickly turned away from an apology to focus on that very trigger point: loss of face. "You shouldn't contradict me in front of others" was his only serious message to her. He knows where he's hot-wired, and like Kate, the young museum manager, he could break the lock between ploy and vulnerability. If he did, what would it look like?

If Stewart still wanted to use humor, he could use it to lighten the moment and disarm his own reaction, instead of using it as a weapon against someone else. Even if humor as a weapon works in ordinary talk, it's a shaky strategy in difficult conversations if others are watching. Stewart could say, "Erica contradicts me when she thinks I'm wrong, no matter who's in the room. We keep a running score of who's right, and I'm usually ahead." Instead of turning his antagonism against Erica, on the premise that his embarrassment is her fault, Stewart would be saving face for himself. Not only is that a more promising tack for getting where he wants to go, but in front of the donors and his boss, it's also a more reliable one.

In this instance, Stewart's response is more mordant than charming. Self-deprecating humor, while attractive to many, is likely to be well out of bounds for someone as concerned with loss of face as Stewart was at the moment. If he thought he had to put himself one-down to change tack, he wouldn't do it. But in this new version, he did change tack, he did lighten the moment, and he did disarm his own reaction. Those were the jobs that needed to be done to get through the moment intact, and he has found a tolerable way to do them. (See more about finding the right words in "The Blueprint for Speaking Well in Tough Moments.")

# The blueprint for speaking well
# in tough moments

Getting down to specifics, how did the people on these pages get the new language they used? They had a blueprint in common for saying what they wanted to say, without either suppressing themselves or falling overboard emotionally. It's a simple blueprint, because in anxious situations, it's hard to remember something complicated at the same time that you're trying to talk.

Clear content

Neutral tone

Temperate phrasing

While the blueprint is simple to grasp, it can be hard to apply if your habit is to be tough or soft, to be blunt or circumspect, to attack or say nothing, to be stubborn or give in, to retaliate or take the punch. In tough conversations, clarity, neutrality, and temperance take practice.

### Clear content

Clear content means let your words do your work for you. Say what you mean. Unfortunately, it's particularly hard to stay with clear content when the news is bad, because it can seem brutal to us. So we try to soften the content. If you're a senior executive, that means saying things like, "Well, Patrick, we're still not sure yet what's going to happen with this job, but in the future, we'll keep our eyes open." That's a roundabout and misleading way to tell someone he didn't get the promotion he hoped for.

Yet there is nothing inherently brutal about honesty. It's not the content, but the manner of delivering the news that makes it brutal or humane. Ask a surgeon; ask a priest; ask a cop. A clear message, neutrally given, can still be tolerable—even though the news is bad.

When a senior executive clearly and neutrally tells a manager, "Patrick, the promotion has gone to someone else," the news is likely to hurt, and the appropriate reaction is sadness, anger, and anxiety. But if the content is clear, the listener can start to deal with the information, not guess at it or misunderstand it. In that way, clear content makes the burden lighter for the counterpart rather than heavier.

### Neutral tone

Tone is the nonverbal part of the message we're delivering. It's the inflection, facial expression, and conscious and unconscious body language that carries emotional weight in a difficult conversation. When Ross said to Jackie during his performance review, "Are you feeling a little overwhelmed, Jackie? In over your head?" it was his tone that made his questions sarcastic rather than sympathetic. It's hard to use a neutral tone when our emotions are running high, but it's a familiar tone to hear: even in crisis, we're accustomed to the classic neutrality of NASA communications: "Houston, we have a problem." It takes practice to acquire that kind of neutrality—in voice, face, and body. But it's part of middle ground, and it helps you both speak well and get heard without distortion.

### Temperate phrasing

In difficult conversation, when you say to yourself, "I can't say *that*," remember that your job is to keep your content clear. So you probably can say that; you just can't say it *that way*. The English language has a huge vocabulary, and there are lots of ways to say what you need to say. Some are soft or vague; some are temperate; some baldly provoke your counterpart with loaded language. If your counterpart dismisses, resists, or throws back your words, he or she is not likely to hold on to your content. When Jackie told Ross, "I've heard that some department managers are unhappy with the way you come across when you're making your recommendations. They think you're kind of cocky and superior. You need to work on your interpersonal

*continued*

skills," even we, who are not in the difficult conversation ourselves, can pick out the loaded language. For Ross, it was like a red flag to a bull.

If Jackie had changed her language—not her content—she might have said, "The managers you audit tell me that your recommendations would go down better if they were delivered colleague-to-colleague, not up-down. It's hard for them to hear about mistakes in their procedures, even when they know you're right." Her goal was to advance the conversation, to hear and be heard accurately, and to have a functional exchange between two people on a sensitive issue. Temperate phrasing will get her there, and provocative phrasing won't.

Clear content, neutral tone, and temperate phrasing are a package deal. For instance, you won't get the same good results if you use temperate phrasing but mix your message with a lot of contradictory body language. Nor will you get a good result if you think your content is too blunt and so you soften it. That's a mix-up. Bluntness is a characteristic of intemperate phrasing, not of content. So softening your content to fix a problem of phrasing won't get you where you want to go. Keep the blueprint simple, and stick with it.

Stewart shared more with Erica than he might like to admit. Erica was off the mark when she bought into the idea that she had to be hypernice to avoid being offensive. If Stewart saw himself as tough but fair when other people consistently saw him as a bully, he was off the mark, too. Of course, Stewart was not as stuck near the passive pole as Erica was. On the contrary, he was caught up in aggressive retaliation, and although he tried to hide it, it cost him a lot.

But he could look for middle ground between deferring to Erica's information and retaliating against it. He might say, "I think you're wrong, but let's see if we can reconcile these different points of view." In fact, half of those words were his boss Gordon's words, and Gordon was seeking to end the confrontation by moving to middle ground. Stewart could move *himself* to middle ground and carry the conversation with him into better balance. It would be a real coup for his reputation if he did.

If he responded to his own emotional triggers by finding balance, Stewart would not simply be tweaking his tough-but-fair style or the iron fist in the velvet glove until they worked as he planned. Of course, those options are always available—there is always more than one tack to take. But it's hard to solve an emotional problem with a combat reaction. Rather than fine-tuning the combat reaction, we're looking for a sea change in the way Stewart handles this kind of conversation.

As always, the more committed Stewart is to the combat model of difficult conversations—the more he sees them as zero-sum battles with one winner and one loser—the less he's going to feel like moving to middle ground. But when the cost of his combat style comes home to him, he might be ready for a change.

If Stewart looked beyond his one style, he would gain a lot of flexibility he now lacks and he would increase his chances of a good outcome. Like Kate, Stewart might find that the scale of his emotional reaction actually shrinks as he gets more skillful. Or maybe it won't; maybe he will always be angry and embarrassed if he's contradicted in front of others. But if he can change tack rather than dig in deeper when his first reaction starts to harm him, he won't get locked in by a ploy that triggers his reaction.

Even with three new tactics—finding middle ground, immunizing, and changing tack—there's one special category of skill that we all need, either for balance or for self-protection, in case we do overreact to a thwarting ploy. We need to know how to recover if something goes wrong.

## Fourth tactic: Recover from blunders and fouls

If we can find middle ground, immunize against thwarting ploys, and change tack, why would we need to know much about recovering from mistakes? For starters, we probably will still make our share of mistakes. If these conversations were easy to get right on the first try, we wouldn't think of them as difficult to begin with. Also, there will be at least two people in the conversation, one of whom may not have our range of skills. On the one hand, we need to be able to recover from what they throw at us. On the other, we need to recover from what *they* see as our mistake, whether we agree or not, since they are likely to give us a hard time if we don't make it right. And finally, we're less likely to overreact to the counterpart who is giving us a hard time, or overreact to the mistake itself, if we know how to recover from it. Being able to recover is an important way to loosen the grip of our own emotions. Recovery—rebalancing anything one person or the other says that is likely to derail the conversation—is the best antidote to derailment. That sounds good, yet it's uncommon to see people recover well from blunders and fouls. Why?

We don't simply struggle to recover from our mistakes; we resist acknowledging them at all. Particularly for people caught up in a combat mentality, admitting a mistake looks like a sign of weakness. For example, rather than dig himself out of trouble, Stewart dug himself in deeper because, to him, admitting a mistake was as good as saying, "I'm guilty; you win."

At the same time, our habits stand in the way. If, the last time someone accused us of a mistake, we either knuckled under or shut down, we may very well do one of those again the next time. For example, Erica's habit, when Stewart bullied her, was to stay near the passive end of the range of response. This time, when he bullied her in front of donors who mattered, Erica didn't want to knuckle under, so she took the only other choice she was familiar with—she shut down and did nothing. That wasn't a very good recovery by any measure, but Erica's habitual range of response was too narrow to give her much scope of action.

More importantly, if we don't agree that we even made a mistake, but someone accuses us, isn't the accusation just a thwarting ploy? Erica didn't think she had made a mistake on her side to begin with, and Stewart didn't think he had, either. If they even acknowledge the so-called mistake, won't they be backing down to a ploy? Anyone would resist doing that; backing down doesn't look very much like a good save.

And there lie the two biggest impediments to recovering from mistakes in difficult conversations: the old zero-sum idea that to acknowledge a mistake is a misplaced kind of deference to an antagonist just when our own self-respect is on the line. And the erroneous idea that to acknowledge a mistake (whether we thought we caused it or not) will neither help us recover from it nor help us rebalance a derailing conversation. Back down to someone like Erica, who has embarrassed Stewart publicly? Defer to a bully like Stewart? If that's how we see it, of course, none of us would make an effort to recover from a mistake—unless we were seriously threatened. As it happened, Erica and Stewart's failure to put their conversation back on the rails did result in serious threats: first, Stewart publicly threatened Erica's job, humorously or not, and next, his boss Gordon threatened Stewart's.

There's a lot on the line. But we've seen people drop ploys that weren't working and pick up new techniques with much better odds of success, even when their emotions were kicking up a storm and their counterparts were making things worse. In the same way, we can master good recoveries, even when our emotions and our counterpart are giving us trouble—although we don't have to reserve recovery as a tactic only for very dire circumstances. Whatever the case, for recovery we need a strategy with four characteristics:

- It will help us rebalance ourselves and the conversation.

- It won't jeopardize our self-respect or our reputation.

- It won't worsen the relationship.

- It can be done unilaterally.

The point is to acknowledge mistakes *for the specific purpose* of recovering from them. Good acknowledgments are disarming: sometimes we want to disarm a ploy our counterpart is using, and sometimes we want to disarm our own reactions. Let's look at examples of both.

### Erica: Disarming Stewart's ploy

If Erica wanted to disarm Stewart's demeaning remarks, she could say something as simple as, "Enough about me. Let's look again at the information these folks need."

If we hold that reply against our criteria, how is Erica doing? To begin with, she's doing about the best job of finding balance that she could in those circumstances. Yes, she's in the grip of her emotions, but she's not reacting to them or to Stewart; instead, she's refocusing the conversation to rebalance it. Her self-respect is intact, and her reputation isn't suffering. She hasn't made her relationship with Stewart any worse, although he may not like that she isn't reacting according to his scenario. And, of course, she has unilaterally picked how she wants to recover, without involving Stewart or anyone else in the room.

The unilateral part is especially important. Stewart was actively disrespecting Erica. While Erica can't compel his respect, she can, as always, bring self-respect to her recovery on her own. What she says now is not dependent on what Stewart has said. She is neither disrespecting him back nor deferring to him. She has, in fact, gone to middle ground between those two, and she has gone there unilaterally.

Acting unilaterally in difficult conversations doesn't mean that it's all about us. Erica isn't so focused on herself that she defends or counterattacks, either of which would pull her into the heat of Stewart's remarks. Acting unilaterally means we accept that we can't control what our counterpart does. So while we will take what he or she does into consideration—we don't ignore it—we're *independent* of what our counterpart does. Acting unilaterally means we can respond with an eye to our own reputation.

But how would Erica come up with that kind of response? First, remember that in Erica's original version, she shut down, not out of deference to Stewart, but because she was blindsided by his offense. Yet Erica has had enough experience with Stewart to know about his bullying ways, and she would have done better to expect an offense and to immunize herself. We want to be self-aware enough to know where we're vulnerable, but building that awareness doesn't take endless self-analysis. Much of it simply involves making explicit our own tacit knowledge about what has given us trouble in hard talks before.

In this new version of the conversation, Erica takes what Stewart has said and goes to the midpoint between a passive response and an aggressive one. She "talks to the ploy," and she does so according to the blueprint—clearly, neutrally, and temperately. Erica's response, "Enough about me," unilaterally calls a halt to this conversation about her, not through sarcasm, appeasement, or retaliation, but by *not* reacting to the ploy. Like the virus that can't latch on to a cell, a ploy that doesn't get a reaction is shut out and shut down.

And then, Erica changes tack. When she says, "Let's look again at the information these folks need," she refocuses the conversation away from Stewart's remarks about her and back to the shared issue between them and, by the way, the one issue that involves everyone in the room. It takes the focus—and the pressure—off the two of them, and it's the best place to look for balance in a conversation that has gone awry.

But, we may wonder through all of this, what has happened to Erica's emotional blaze? Nothing specific. As Mamet says, "you learn to act in spite of what you are feeling." Emotions don't evaporate in difficult conversations, but they are harnessed by skill. The grip that big emotions have on us loosens as skill leads us to better outcomes.

Erica's recovery from Stewart's ploy doesn't come from a list of specific answers to specific provocations, like matching one from column A to one from column B. There are several decisions she could make about how she wants to handle the moment. She could take a joint focus on what Stewart has just done and on the landscape of the conversation itself by saying, "We have two problems here. One is the strategy for this campaign. The other is that we're so far apart on how to handle it that we're even far apart on how to talk about it." Or, if she wanted to focus exclusively on Stewart's remark, she could say, "I understand what you just said, but I don't know how to read it." In each case, she would find her own words, and to recover from Stewart's foul, she would consistently apply the same basic techniques of going to middle ground, immunizing, and changing direction when the first tack she took didn't work. Even with spectators in the room.

### Stewart: Disarming his own reaction

Erica had to recover from Stewart's ploy, but Stewart himself was in a stickier situation. Out of anger and embarrassment, he may have gone too far in his reaction to Erica's contradiction. But he didn't want to back down then and lose face even more. Stewart needed to recover from his own bad reaction—he had to get himself out of what he had gotten himself into.

While there's always more than one tack to take, the fastest and easiest way to recover from a mistake of our own is to learn how to acknowledge it well. That would be hard for Stewart, because he brought a combat mentality to situations like this one. He believed that if he acknowledged a mistake, he made himself small; he'd look like a loser. Is he right? That depends on how he handles it. The biggest disadvantage to the fear that acknowledging fault diminishes our stature is that it leads either to stonewalling or to lousy acknowledgments. Both hurt our reputations, not to mention our relationships, as much as the original blunder does. So it will help Stewart if he changes his mind about what he's trying to do.

If he gets away from the idea that acknowledging a mistake makes him look small, he can get to the idea that, if he handles it well, an acknowledgment makes him look good. It enhances his reputation. He can afford this. And, as a very important side benefit in this case, acknowledging a mistake would let him regain his balance in the conversation, instead of sinking deeper into trouble.

We know that Stewart had a combat model of difficult conversation, so it makes sense that he leaned more toward tough than soft when he talked to a subordinate. But here again, the reason Stewart got stuck at tough, even when he was in front of an audience of significant people and he could see the conversation degenerating as he talked on, is that he saw only two polar choices—tough or soft. And he had already put soft out of bounds, principally because he didn't want to get involved in touchy-feely, weak-looking responses. Fair enough: soft doesn't look good to him. But that still leaves middle ground.

Yet once Stewart had dug himself in so deep, wasn't it too late to back out? How could he get the conversation back on the rails? Simply put, Stewart could change tack—right in the middle of his joke. Just as he paused and looked at Erica before he started in with the joking remarks, he could pause again now, look at her, and—taking a page from Fiorello LaGuardia—say, "When I make a mistake, it's a beaut." If Stewart wants to point out that he meant his last remark as a joke, he could say, "That may have gone past funny. When I make a mistake, it's a beaut."

That's a good, neutral acknowledgment—not tough, not soft. Without question, Stewart could take a step like that unilaterally and with no loss of face. It's true that Erica might not warm to him instantly, but he would salvage his reputation with Gordon and the donors. However, we know that Stewart was angry and embarrassed, so where did an acknowledgment like that come from? Did he pull it out of the air?

Probably not. When he immunizes himself against his vulnerability to being contradicted in front of others, Stewart would do well to come up right then with a couple of hip-pocket phrases—comments that he, like Kate, the young museum senior manager, could tuck away and then pull out and use when he's caught in a bad moment. To expect to come up with a good response in a trigger situation is gambling against the odds; to prepare ahead of time for a known vulnerability is good judgment and good technique.

### Gordon: Disarming the moment

Gordon saw the fiasco unfolding in front of him as an "I can't go there" conversation. It looked too delicate and difficult for him to manage. But Gordon did have the skill he needed to handle the moment. How do we know? Because he used it when he spoke to Stewart privately, after the onlookers had left the room. At that point, he turned to Stewart and said, "I think you've crossed a line."

When he and Stewart spoke alone, Gordon used the blueprint—he was clear, neutral, and temperate. He could have used the blueprint to say the same thing in front of the others. An audience changed how Gordon *felt* he could handle the conflict; it didn't deactivate his skills. David Mamet says, "Remember, you do not have to feel like performing your action. Your skills become habitual." If Gordon changed his frame of mind about difficult conversations with an audience—if he looked at them as unfortunate situations, yes, but not abnormal ones—he would bring his skills to bear and manage the conversation just as he managed it with Stewart alone. He might continue to feel angry and embarrassed, but he no longer has to fear mishandling the situation itself. He does know what to do.

## Coming together

Emotions are very real players in difficult conversation. Together with tough personalities and prickly issues, disruptive emotions define difficult conversations for most of us. If we focus in a little closer, however, the real problem is the match-up of *their* thwarting ploys and *our* points of vulnerability.

If we have no immunity, can't put our feet on middle ground, get stuck on the wrong tack, can't recover—and our counterparts' ploys have a lock on our vulnerabilities—then we're in trouble. We can't move forward in the conversation if we get swallowed up by our own emotions or react to our counterparts' provocations. We'll either go toe to toe, trying to score off each other, or our counterpart will play us like a fish as we rise to the bait every time, or we'll save both of us the trouble and just shut down.

Instead, it helps to think of thwarting ploys as countering moves in a chess game, which is largely what they are. It makes sense in chess that our counterpart isn't intent on making things go smoothly for us. Likewise, it makes sense in chess that we don't play into our counterpart's moves, but aim to neutralize them and move past them. If we think of thwarting ploys as typical, albeit objectionable, moves that we don't want to react to emotionally, we can engage our brain, not just our gut, when we handle them.

In fact, if we focus more closely still, the true heart of the problem is the small stock of skills we have on our side for dealing with the inevitable emotional stresses that go with difficult conversations. But we don't have to face them with so little at hand. And, while emotions will always be on the scene, they don't have to be the lead players. Four skills—finding midpoint in the range of response, immunizing against our known vulnerabilities, learning to change tack, and knowing how to recover from error—let us think how we want to respond, not just react. That alone will put us way ahead.

These are techniques for dealing with how we know we feel and with the incoming emotional ploys that we know we're vulnerable to. But there are other challenges that we can't prepare for in the same way, because we don't know—we can't know—what they are. What can we do about what we can't see?

# Remember:

- With good tactics, we can respond in tough conversations without being hamstrung by our emotions. We'll still have our emotions, but we'll go forward on skill.

- Finding middle ground lets us decide which way we want to move from the center, not from the emotional extremes.

- Immunizing ourselves against thwarting ploys lets us protect ourselves where we're vulnerable, instead of just reacting to the ploys that trigger us.

- Changing tack gives us different ways to handle what's amiss in a tough conversation, instead of repeating a small stock of tactics whether they work or not.

- Recovering from mistakes is a skill that lets us get past our own rough spots, instead of watching our mistakes take over the conversation.

## CHAPTER 10

# Working Blind in the "Breakdown Gap"

GIL'S SCHOOL AND Delia's school had recently merged. Easygoing, affable Gil stepped down as chairman of his school's social studies department, and young, well-educated Delia stepped in as head of the merged departments. As the members of the formerly separate departments began to get comfortable with each other in meetings, some ribbing went back and forth over how each department used to handle particular questions in American history, with each side noisily defending their favored approach. Now that he didn't have to act as chairman, Gil liked to join in with the others. Delia, now chairman, did not.

After one of those meetings, Delia took Gil aside and spoke quietly but clearly. "It doesn't matter how fuzzy you think Mary's ideas are," she said. "These attacks on her have to stop."

Gil looked at Delia with blank astonishment. "Attacks on Mary?" he sputtered. "I *like* Mary!"

Delia said nothing more.

Later, Gil hoped that the surprising confrontation had been a simple misunderstanding and, he hoped somewhat uneasily, one that had been cleared up.

Nevertheless, he felt there was tension between the two of them, and it occurred to Gil that Delia might think she needed to assert extra authority over him. He was aware that it could be hard to be the new chair, especially in a merger, when the former chair is always around. Gil was not sorry to give up the chairman's chores, and he wanted to let Delia know that she could relax and count on him for his knowledge and experience.

So the next day he handed Delia some papers and told her in his offhand way, "I've cobbled together a few notes for you about some of the decisions we made in the old department. Now you'll have the deep background on us. I've drunk beer and argued with this lot for years. I know them better than their grandparents did. Ask me anything you need to know."

Without glancing at the papers, Delia said, "You've been here a long time, Gil, and we'll be raising the bar for everyone. I'll be observing your classes. I hope you can stretch yourself. I'm sure you probably can."

Gil felt like he had been slapped; Delia walked away.


## How does it happen?

Clearly, this is a situation in which at least one person is baffled by a confrontation he didn't see coming. We've already seen conversations turn toxic when the combat mentality and big emotions come into play. In both cases, we may not like it, but we can usually see what's going wrong. But that's not true when our conversation is falling apart because of a breakdown over misconceptions—a breakdown between what one side means and what the other side hears. What I call the *breakdown gap* is the split that opens between counterparts, the gap in which the most complicated parts of a tough conversation take place in darkness. We can't see how our counterparts are taking what we say, and then how they feel in reaction. As a result, both sides form misconceptions based on their own perspectives, unable to see why their counterpart's reactions are so unreasonable. Conversations fail over complications in the breakdown gap in a particularly damaging way—with both sides making harsh judgments about the other.

When we look at these conversations from the outside, though, it's often easy to see why they might break down—it's even easy to see how to put the conversation back on track. Why can't the people in the conversation see? There are three reasons tied up together, and we've seen two of them before. First, the combat mentality gets in the way. People can't see what's wrong in the breakdown gap if they think they hear sabers rattling. Like Gil, when he was first confronted by Delia, they are quick to wonder, "What's happening? Is this a fight?" and that claims all their attention. Second, it makes sense that people's emotions will cloud their vision. It makes sense that Delia takes Gil's comments about his connections as a challenge—even if she's wrong—simply because she is anxious about asserting her new authority.

The third reason that the people involved can't see what's breaking down between them is that difficult conversations operate on two levels: communication up top and interpretation running underneath. Both sides know what's happening on the top level—they know what each side says. But neither side knows for sure what's happening on the lower level—what their counterpart intends or how their counterpart perceives them (although, right or wrong, people often think they know). It's in the gap between intentions on one side and perceptions on the other that the most notorious breakdowns occur (see "Complications in the Breakdown Gap").

## Complications in the breakdown gap

Figuring out what's wrong in the breakdown gap is a complicated business. But it starts simply enough.

In any conversation, people take turns being speaker and listener. We can freeze a moment in time, with Gil, the former social studies department chair, as the speaker, and Delia, the new chair, as the listener. On Gil's side, there's a bright line, with what he *says* above it where Delia can hear it, and what he *intends* below it where Delia cannot see. On Delia's side, below the bright line is what she *perceives* to be going on, and Gil cannot see what she perceives. Above the line is what Delia *says* in reaction. (At the moment she reacts, their roles change: Delia becomes the speaker and Gil the listener.)

In real conversation, Delia only has access to what Gil *says*. If Gil's words accurately match up with his intentions (and if Delia believes him), then Delia does know what Gil's intentions are, through Gil's words. She *perceives* that what he says is what he means.

That would be the case if Gil said, "We may have a shared problem here: shifting departmental authority from one of us to the other. I don't know how we're going to work it out, but I'm comfortable trying. I have some ideas I'd like to run by you to see what you think."

If Gil is masking his intentions with a mixed message, however—or if Delia doesn't believe that Gil's words line up with his intentions—then Delia can only *guess* at Gil's intentions. That might be the case if Gil had said, "We have a shared problem with shifting departmental authority from one of us to the other. I'm sure we can work it out together. Here are the changes I'm looking for from you. That should do it."

When Delia guesses, she makes what she can—or what she wants—of Gil's intentions. In this second case, she might guess, "When Gil says, 'work it out together,' he really means, 'Delia makes all the changes. Delia gives in. I win, Delia loses.'" That's Delia's *perception* of what's going on. In *reaction*, she might say, "I don't have a problem with my own authority, although you might. I have no intention of taking instruction from you."

Is this what Gil meant? Hard to tell. In fact, Gil may not have thought through his intentions at all. But that could be Delia's *perception*.

In difficult conversations, it doesn't always happen that Gil *tells* Delia his intentions—tells her the whole truth—and that Delia buys it. That's where the conversation begins to break down. What goes on is even more complicated than this snippet of conversation makes it sound because the breakdown is not happening up above the bright line on the blue-sky communications level, but underground, where people, like Delia, are not so much *listening* as they are trying to *interpret*—that is, guess.

The breakdown is also complicated because most well-intentioned people, like Gil, believe that their counterpart is *reacting* to their own good *intentions*, almost independent of what they *say*. That's why you will hear people protest, "I don't know what happened. I meant well," even when they're standing in the rubble of a failed conversation.

But Delia is not reacting to Gil's intentions. She is not even reacting directly to Gil's *words*. Delia is *reacting* to what she *perceives* is the intention behind Gil's words.

In fact, people who are in Delia's position and are reacting to how they perceive their counterpart's intentions often do brush aside the counterpart's words. They assume that his words don't match what he really intends—but not in the favorable way that Gil might imagine. They do not assume that his intentions are good regardless of his words. On the contrary, they often think that the words are ploys designed to cover up very questionable intentions. Why? Because in difficult conversation, very often that's true—the words are half true and half misleading. To make a complicated situation worse, once Delia has set aside Gil's words, her interpretation of Gil's intentions is frequently wrong, because the more difficult the conversation, the worse a guesser Delia is likely to be.

*continued*

And then, Gil and Delia will change places, with Delia speaking and Gil listening. At that point, the mix of *intentions*, *words*, *perceptions*, and *reactions* becomes twice as complicated. It's no wonder there's a breakdown gap between the two sides, however well intentioned they may be.

It's very uncomfortable to be caught in conversations that are as unexpectedly complicated and hard to read as the two that Gil faced. Something had broken down between what Gil, and Delia too, were trying to do and how their counterpart took it. What happened there?

### Breakdown between intentions and perceptions on *two* sides

When Delia accused Gil of attacking Mary, Gil felt as if Delia were attacking *him*. Immediately, Gil leaped to the defense of his good intentions: he liked Mary; he had no intention of attacking her. But there's an unseen complication here. By putting all the weight of his defense on his intentions alone, Gil implied that Delia clearly misinterpreted his intentions toward Mary.

In that simple view, Gil was right and Delia was wrong. With that view, all Gil would need to do is tell Delia that his intentions were good, Delia would believe him, and she would see that she had simply taken him the wrong way. Problem solved. There's nothing wrong with Gil's reasoning, but it is not likely to get him the outcome he wants. Why not? Because Delia's view was identical to Gil's—but in reverse.

Delia believed that her own intentions—standing up for Mary—were the good intentions here. She thought that her own perceptions of Gil's comments to Mary were accurate. In Delia's eyes, *she* was right and *Gil* was wrong, not the other way around. To Delia, Gil's self-defense now looked like another thwarting ploy—just like his attacks on Mary in the first place. The conversation did not look like a simple misinterpretation to Delia, at least not a mistake on her side.

The breakdown here happened, as breakdowns always do, on the interpretation level running underneath the communication level. There was a breakdown between intentions and perceptions on two sides, not a problem of right on one side and wrong on the other.

### Breakdown between intentions and words on *one* side

In their second conversation, Gil added a different complication. Again, he believed his intentions were good when he offered his experience, connections, and knowledge as support for Delia in her new role. But Delia surprised him by dashing cold water on those intentions. What happened there?

Gil genuinely didn't intend to unsettle Delia, but he did give her a mixed message. Even though he had an idea that she was uneasy with her new authority, Gil meant both to be supportive of her and to showcase his own strengths. In a simple view, Delia would weigh the two messages as Gil intended—with the main emphasis on his support and then a separate acknowledgment of his experience. But that didn't happen.

The problem here is that Gil knew where Delia was vulnerable, and yet he closed his eyes to the most likely way she would read the mix: as an outward show of support and a covert challenge. So, based on how Delia read Gil's words, she responded with a mixed message of her own: a pointed warning coupled with tepid support.

## Oversimplification and the delusion of good intentions

This gets complicated, so these conversations practically beg to be simplified. And we understandably want to oblige when everything

is so murky. But that would be a mistake. Although it's always easier to oversimplify any tough conversation, it's risky to assume, as
Gil did, that because he meant well, the trouble between Delia and
him was probably a simple misunderstanding on her side—certainly not a difficulty on his. That assumption is what I call the *delusion of good intentions* at work.

The real problem is the next step: when we oversimplify a
complicated conversation and the delusion of good intentions
clears us of blame, we stop there. But if we stop—and just sidestep the thorny parts of a tough conversation—we can't right what
is going wrong. We can only add to the confusion in the breakdown gap and, time and again, alienate our counterparts.

## Justices Burger and Blackmun:
## A high-level breakdown

Even powerful and long-standing relationships can falter over
complications in the breakdown gap. Linda Greenhouse, in her
Pulitzer Prize–winning biography, *Becoming Justice Blackmun*, de-
scribes the fraying of a friendship between Warren Burger, chief
justice of the Supreme Court, and Harry Blackmun, associate justice of the Supreme Court. Their friendship had begun in kinder-
garten and had been constant for sixty-six years.[1] When Burger
first became chief justice in Washington and Blackmun was still an
appeals court judge in Missouri, they wrote to each other about
their deep sense of partnership. "My support is yours for the asking at all times," Blackmun wrote to Burger.[2] And Burger wrote,
"I want your ideas . . . I never sought this job—never really would
want it—but now it is here & *we will do it*."[3] During that time,
Burger consistently looked to Blackmun for advice. And when
Blackmun joined him on the Supreme Court, Burger rejoiced.

Despite their long and close relationship, however, when they
served together on the Supreme Court, a rift opened between

Burger and Blackmun and continued to widen. The principle problem appeared to be that the two of them did not look at the issues before the court in the same way. According to Greenhouse, "There appeared to be no basis on which they could constructively discuss, let alone overcome, their doctrinal differences."[4]

Friends from the age of five, and no way to talk together about their differences? In fact, Burger and Blackmun had anticipated having different points of view. But each perhaps had an unrealistically simple view of what would happen between them when a difference arose. "Whatever you do," wrote Blackmun to Burger, "there will be no hard feeling between the two of us and no need ever to explain or defend."[5] But there were hard feelings. And although Burger had written, "I will welcome—indeed I invite—your suggestions," the chief justice was offended when Blackmun's suggestions arrived.[6]

The breakdown between Burger and Blackmun was profound and was made up of problems that are familiar to us—but that are not simple. Yes, there were abrasive "doctrinal differences" between the two men, but those differences are the stock in trade of many court benches. More problematically, the differences occurred in a context in which partnership and the tension between one-up and one-down were blurred—they were colleagues, of course, but at the same time, it was Justice Blackmun and *Chief* Justice Burger. There were also mixed messages between them—but each side expected the other to read and weigh the different parts of the messages correctly. That blurring abetted, and those expectations couldn't stop, the breakdowns between what each man said and what the other made of it.

Complications like these chipped away at Burger and Blackmun's years of common ground, and the gap between them widened until, over the course of the rest of their lives, they were unable to bridge it. Instead of seeing and fixing the problems in the breakdown gap, they watched their long and vibrant conversation close down into silence.

# The slippery slope of misconceptions

How do difficult conversations start to break down over misconceptions in practice? It begins harmlessly enough. Early on, when a conversation may be hard but still looks promising, almost everyone tries to look at a problem evenhandedly, from both sides' points of view. But a conversation starts to go wrong if, instead of meeting us halfway, our counterpart does something we don't expect.

In Gil and Delia's case, each side pushed back instead of meeting halfway. Taking the slant that he was right and Delia was wrong about his demeanor toward Mary, Gil went straight to defense. In the next round, deciding that Gil was hiding a challenge behind his support, Delia went straight to offense. But since we can't see (and don't talk about) a breakdown between intentions and perceptions on the interpretation level, an unexpected reaction leads to full-blown misconceptions about our counterpart and the direction of the conversation itself. The next slippery step into the breakdown gap begins when we start actively, if innocently, covering up.

## Cover-ups

In tough conversations, we want to cover up a lot of things, like emotions we hope to hide and ploys we don't want to own up to. We cover up by choosing words or stratagems that are at odds with our meaning. When Gil was telling Delia about his long familiarity with his colleagues, he wanted her to hear the supportive part of his message while he concealed the self-promoting part. His cover-up wasn't seamless, though. Enough self-promotion showed through it to make Delia try to decipher what was going on behind his words.

Counterparts are constantly trying to figure out what we mean *despite* what we say. If they suspect a cover-up, they take less and less of what we say at face value. In fact, for good reasons, our counterparts often think we are willfully distorting what we mean, because to some degree we are. And they do the same thing when they're talking.

This is a sequence—covering up on one side and trying to see through the cover-up on the other—that almost guarantees misunderstanding. Even worse, cover-ups feed into a larger pattern of evasive talk.

### Don't ask, don't tell

Difficult conversations seem to have their own unwritten "don't ask, don't tell" operating policy. Repeatedly in these chapters, we've seen tough conversations in which people's emotions and ploys have been belied by their words. But until those conversations have been revised, we have never heard anyone talk about the breakdown between the emotions and intentions on their side and the words they say to their counterparts. Neither side will say anything about how the conversation itself is affecting them, no matter how worried, baffled, or offended people become. Like Delia, they might raise the tension with a veiled threat. Or like Gil, they might simply react with stunned surprise. But they will not talk—nor will they ask—about what is making the conversation break down a little more each time one side or the other speaks. Why not?

For one reason, we are determined to stay on track—we want to get the conversation over with, not deconstruct it. And we specifically want to avoid talking about personal, squishy perceptions when we might be wrong—with no blueprint for talking about a conversation in trouble, what would we say to what we might hear? As a result, what's going wrong in the conversation remains undiscussable, while misconceptions thrive.

### Damaging judgments

Cover-ups and "don't ask, don't tell" wouldn't be so damaging to conversations if the two sides didn't take one further step. With no good way to talk about the problems in the conversation itself, yet wrestling to interpret the intentions behind a sinking conversation, both sides begin to make judgments that reflect poorly on the other person: we think a conversation is going badly *because* of the counterpart's bad intentions, while at the same time, we think a conversation goes badly *in spite* of our own good intentions.

At that point, the biggest problem with cover-ups and a "don't ask, don't tell" policy may be what happens when we give them up. People drop their cover-ups when they believe their counterparts have pushed them too far. And, once dropped, any cover-up looks as if it were meant to be manipulative. Now people *will* talk about what's happening in the conversation. Tossing aside both cover-ups and "don't ask, don't tell," people attack each others' intentions or ploys. We are back in full combat mode, and each side believes that the other is finally showing his or her true colors.

Afterward, what stays in both counterparts' minds is the nadir of the conversation, when each person felt misunderstood, embattled, offended, and falsely accused. Yet each side also judges this low point as the counterpart's most naked, honest moment. Self-justification rises on both sides. Respect crumbles. Eventually, neither side *wants* to build a bridge across the breakdown gap—who would?

The breakdowns between Gil and Delia are partly failures of skill and partly an absence of skill. Cover-ups and "don't ask, don't tell" will stand in for skill when we can't manage the split between intentions and perceptions. And breakdowns will happen when we have no skill at all for dealing with the single most complicating factor in tough conversations—that there is so much we cannot see.

Misconceptions, cover-ups, "don't ask, don't tell," and harsh judgments all happened to Melissa and Tracy in the next chapter as they stumbled blindly into one pitfall after another. Neither one had bad intentions. Neither one could see how confusing their two conversations would become or how much damage they would do. And neither one had the skill—good strategy and tactics—to put the conversations right.

## Remember:

- The worst complications in tough conversations happen—unseen—in the breakdown gap between what one side intends and what the other side perceives.

- Oversimplifying tough conversations and the delusion of good intentions let us keep our distance from real complications—and then we can't right what is wrong.

- Both sides cover up emotions, intentions, ploys, and confusion itself. But each side constantly tries to see through the cover-ups, suspicious of what is hidden.

- Both sides fall into a "don't ask, don't tell" pattern, so what is going wrong in the conversation is unmentionable.

- With both sides mum about what they intend and what they think, confusion, tension, and suspicion mount until respect collapses and we slide back into conversational warfare.

## CHAPTER 11

# Out of the Breakdown Gap

## *Strategy and Tactics*

TRACY, THE FINANCIAL administration officer of a research center, banged into her office, muttering angrily to herself, without even glancing at Drew, her staff assistant and office mate. It was the end of the fiscal year, which was always a hectic time. But to make things truly frantic, Tracy had just learned that Fisk, one of the program managers, was about to miss an important grant deadline because his numbers were in disarray. Now Tracy was supposed to swoop in like Red Adair and put out the fire and, of course, not miss her own fiscal year deadlines. Angry and resentful about the extra burden of work, she didn't try to hide her temper.

By the end of the day, Drew hadn't spoken to Tracy at all, but had again gone around Tracy to their boss, Melissa, the research center's associate director, because working next to Tracy was so difficult when she was in this mood. Drew never talked about Tracy's annoyed and self-important manner to Tracy herself, because she was so short-tempered with him, and he was uncomfortable with her personality even at easier times.

Melissa had had her own run-ins with Tracy—everyone in the office had. Melissa said, "I can't say our working relationship is close. Tracy is great with the numbers but not with the people skills. She's pretty aggravating. But I can say that I'm sympathetic right now. Fisk has given her a big problem at a bad time. Even so, I can't have Tracy contributing to tension and low morale in the office, especially if Drew will be working a lot of overtime to get through this crunch. And I can't have Drew running to me every afternoon. So I'll talk to her.

"But it is so hard to have a conversation with her. I'm a conceptualizer; methodical thinkers like Tracy drive me nuts. Discussions with Tracy just don't use my time well. I have a hard time hiding my frustration when she backtracks over ground we've already covered. I get irritated when she harps on minute levels of detail and can't see the big picture. Still, I have to put a stop to this moodiness. I've promised myself that I won't get impatient, though. I'll stay mellow."

The next morning, when Tracy got the e-mail that Melissa wanted to talk to her, a red flag went up in Tracy's mind: "If Melissa wants to talk to me, it must be something big. She never has time for the people who report to her. I can't say she's much of an administrator. She likes the 'professorial' side of her job and is very hands-off with everything else. She doesn't want to be involved in administration; she wants it to run itself. And I pretty much make the administrative side run, single-handedly, although no one here seems to appreciate it. This numbers problem with Fisk is just the latest thing dumped on me. There's not enough time for this and everything else. Melissa doesn't understand that. In fact, she doesn't understand the work at all. She thinks things are easy when they're actually very involved. I try to show her that, but she hates details."

Tracy was ready to say no to the new work she assumed Melissa would hand her. But Tracy still had to give herself a pep talk because she had a history of getting confused and losing what she meant to say when a conversation got tough and her emotions were involved. When that happened, she would give in just to get the conversation over with. She did not want to give in on this, so she pumped herself up: "If Melissa wants to talk to me because she's got something else to hand off right now, I'll just tell her that she'll have to handle it herself. She won't dare push too hard. She needs me, and she knows it. This place would collapse if I stopped holding it up."

Melissa waved Tracy to the armchair as soon as Tracy got to her office, fixed coffee for both of them, and settled herself on the couch. Melissa opened calm and low-key: "I want to tell you how grateful I am, Tracy, that you have taken on everything that's come your way. The end of the fiscal year is always intense for you, and Fisk couldn't have picked a worse time to find himself with a numbers crisis. I know Drew will be a great help to you. He has told me he'll put in as much overtime as you need. But we wouldn't be able to get through this without your ability to rise to a challenge when we need you to, and I appreciate it."

Instead of being gratified and put at ease by Melissa's appreciation, Tracy was instantly suspicious. The coffee, the compliment—those weren't Melissa's style. Melissa was sugarcoating something, but Tracy didn't know what. She hated being caught off-guard. It made her nervous when she couldn't read what people were up to. So Tracy pushed aside Melissa's appreciation and turned to what she had prepared during her pep talk to herself.

"I just have to get this off my chest," Tracy began. "The problem here is that there's much more to my job than you have ever been aware of. You'd rather focus on conferences and programs, so you never have time to listen to how financial operations really work, even though they are important. You always want short answers to big questions. For instance, I don't think you understand how much time these grant requirements take. Let me bring you up to date on what's happened just in the last six months." From memory, Tracy began to go through what she knew so well. Step by step, and in detail, she reviewed the demands she had needed to meet in working on the grants, how much harder these demands made it for her to handle the pressures of other financial operations, and how stressful all this was for her.

Tracy was now in the conversational mode that drove Melissa crazy. Melissa's reason for the conversation—the problem Drew had brought to Melissa in the first place—got lost as Tracy drilled down into the minutiae of her job, a great deal of which Melissa actually did know. In fact, not only was Tracy making Melissa impatient, but Tracy's blunt assertion that Melissa didn't understand the work struck Melissa as an offensively condescending way for Tracy to talk to her boss. Still, Melissa had committed to staying mellow, and shutting Tracy down would be harsh. So Melissa swallowed her annoyance and—without being blunt—tried to clue her subordinate in to the tension Tracy was creating in her own office.

"Maybe you're right," Melissa said. "Drew has told me that you can be abrupt when you're under pressure. That's understandable, of course . . ." And right then, Melissa got an idea that took *her* off course, and she began to do what she does best—work with the bigger picture.

Toning herself down to stay mellow, Melissa asked, "Do you think the burden is too much for the two of you as things now stand? If Drew can put in enough extra hours, how would it be if we divide up between you and Drew the two big issues that are on your plate right now? Fisk's problem is the thornier one, and we would depend on your expertise for that. Meanwhile, Drew could handle the year-end work. It will take him more time than it would take you, and he would have to depend on you for advice and some guidance, but he's worked with you on a fiscal year closing before and he might be up to the challenge. I would want your clearance on the plan first," Melissa finished gracefully, "and then I'd propose it to Drew." She was very pleased with a plan that would cut through several problems at once.

Tracy, however, was not. The unexpected idea came at her so quickly that Tracy's mind went blank and she automatically pushed back. "Drew?! He couldn't possibly handle the year-end close. I'd just have to fix the mess he'd make of it. How would that make my job easier?"

Tracy was at first unnerved by the sign that she wasn't completely essential to every job. Then she was struck by the feeling that, for once, she actually could read what Melissa really meant. "Wait a minute," Tracy said. "Is this a demotion? Is that what this is all about?"

Hearing that, Melissa's sympathy completely ran out. Melissa thought to herself, "This is ridiculous. Where in the world did she get that? I hate it when personal paranoia gets twisted up with real issues. Why did I even bother with the soft and mellow? No good deed goes unpunished."

So she said to Tracy, with the old impatience in her tone, "No, Tracy. For heaven's sake, get a grip. There's no plan to demote you." Melissa stood up. "I give up," she said. "Just two things: Stop snarling at Drew. Then, figure out how you're going to handle the work. I'm going to get back to my own work now. Good-bye."

Awkwardly and not at all reassured, Tracy got up and returned to her office.

Once she was out of the heat of the moment, she chewed over what Melissa had said, and as she calmed down, the plan began to look like something that might work. Maybe Melissa was telling the truth when she said there was no intention to promote Drew at Tracy's expense. If Drew put in enough overtime, he probably wouldn't get himself into too much trouble. With just Fisk and his numbers to handle, Tracy could still review Drew, and her work-life balance might even start to make some sense. This could work.

But how to go back to Melissa? Tracy thought maybe she had struck the wrong note in the last conversation and possibly hadn't handled herself in an ideal way. But, she remembered, her previous boss in the corporate world had always said exactly what he wanted to say, no matter how direct, and it seemed to work out for him. Yet, admittedly, it would be hard for Tracy to concede that Melissa could solve a problem in Tracy's own domain. So, again, Tracy wanted to plan out what she was going to say to Melissa. That way, she wouldn't be taken by surprise and wouldn't blank out a second time. Instead, she would just go in there with a lot of confidence and be very professional.

## What's happening here?

Let's stop here for a moment. We've seen this kind of snarly conversation before, but here it is with its breakdowns over misconceptions laid bare. Looking in from the outside, we can say that Melissa and Tracy's problem was that they didn't know their two assumptions about the topic were on separate tracks and, by the way, we might say, if they were really listening, they would see that. Melissa and Tracy themselves, however, would have pointed to the other's insufferable style as the real problem. That's why they couldn't listen any better than they did.

The truth is that even those two issues together—diverging tracks and conflicting styles—didn't sink this conversation. Melissa and Tracy's worst problems were in the patterns of their conversation, although we don't usually see what's breaking down in the conversation itself because we're not looking there.

Both sides were covering up before the conversation even began. Melissa wanted to cover up her usual impatience with Tracy out of sympathy for Tracy's work overload. She consciously chose an opening that was at odds with her message: she intended to talk about an office problem, but she softened her words and her manner to such an unexpected degree that Tracy didn't pick up on the problem with Drew at all. Meanwhile, Melissa couldn't read the intentions behind Tracy's off-track monologue, but what Melissa guessed about them made her suspicious. Yet, she followed the "don't ask, don't tell" policy and never mentioned what she thought. And *still* Melissa covered up, until she finally passed judgment on Tracy—Tracy was paranoid. Then Melissa dropped her cover-up with a thud.

On her side, Tracy wanted to cover up her Achilles' heel. If she got keyed up and blanked out, Melissa would be able to make her back down. As a cover-up, Tracy scripted her part so that she wouldn't have to think on her feet. But confusingly, Melissa *didn't* dump on her subordinate the extra work that Tracy's script had anticipated; Melissa instead sided with her. Tracy knew she didn't read people well when she was caught off guard, so Melissa's sympathetic behavior simply increased Tracy's suspicion. Yet *still* Tracy clung to her script, the only cover-up she had prepared, even as it threw her further off course. "Don't ask, don't tell" was Tracy's policy; she would never admit to being confused or ask for clarification.

Even with these disaster-prone patterns in the conversation, the two of them actually did have a workable plan. And Melissa did end the conversation just as it teetered on the brink of the breakdown gap. Tracy did rethink and decide she had a stake in Melissa's plan. So Melissa and Tracy were going back for a second round. We'll go back, too.

## The end-of-fiscal-year workload agreement, round 2

When she met with Melissa the second time, Tracy was fully prepared. She told Melissa that, yes, she thought Melissa's plan to split the work with Drew was acceptable. To Tracy's relief, Melissa only said, "Fine, go ahead." She didn't seem to gloat that Tracy had backed down. Tracy took confidence from that, and now that she had conceded that Melissa's solution was feasible, Tracy was ready to speak the rest of her piece about her own recurring issue—her crucial role in the department, no matter how reluctant some were to give Tracy her due.

"I realize that some people might have a problem with me for being very organized. They probably think I'm too organized, but I don't care. And I know what you're going to say—that I'm a perfectionist. Well, I am. Maybe that's a bad thing, but that's just who I am."

Melissa was completely baffled by this warp of what she believed she had plainly told Tracy was a problem with her irate behavior toward Drew. For a moment, she simply stared at Tracy. Then Melissa said, "I'm at a loss. I don't have a problem with how organized you are, if that's what you're getting at." Then hearing again what sounded like insolence in Tracy's tone, Melissa looked at her narrowly, "Are you intentionally twisting my words? Are you challenging me?"

Tracy began to feel confused and anxious at the unplanned direction Melissa was taking the conversation she had prepped for. She blurted out, "Yesterday, you said the job was too much of a burden for me."

"No I didn't," Melissa replied testily. "I asked if you and Drew wanted to reorganize the workload to make it less of a burden for *both* of you."

"But what you really meant was that I was too slow."

Finally, at that, Melissa grew incensed. She stood up and leaned across her desk toward Tracy. "Are you calling me a liar?" she demanded.

Tracy couldn't think what to say. She was stopped short by the huge gap between how she had meant the conversation to go and Melissa's furious—and inexplicable—accusation.


## From chain reaction to failure

It is terribly unfortunate that it was not Melissa's proposal—which was satisfactory to both of them—that was left standing when their conversation collapsed. Instead, it was Melissa and Tracy's anger, offensiveness, distortions, and accusations. As a result, their working relationship suffered heavy damage. Of course, word of their meltdown got out, which was hard on their reputations. Respect between them was gone, and each believed the other was personally responsible for what had happened.

That's a very high price to pay, and it reveals a big problem: when we ask what went wrong in a difficult conversation, we point to the wrong things. The problem in these conversations was not one of the usual suspects—poor listening or incompatible styles. Melissa and Tracy had listened to each other and they had tried to read between the lines. Also, they had tried to compensate for their clashing personal styles. Going even further, both sides would have said that they worked hard to make this conversation come out right. In time, they did revert to the combat mentality and they did get caught up in their signature emotions, but they had been working hard not to.

And neither Melissa nor Tracy had bad intentions—it didn't occur to Melissa that her soft opening would make Tracy suspicious, and Tracy didn't mean to go off the rails the way she did and offend Melissa. In fact, both had valid reasons for what they did: Melissa and Tracy covered up, for example, because each thought that her faults would undermine the conversation or wreck her chances of getting a good outcome.

Despite all the effort and good intentions, what sent this conversation into breakdown was a chain reaction that we've seen before in chapter 10, a chain reaction in the way Melissa and Tracy were handling the conversation itself—from covering up, to "don't ask, don't tell," to judging each other at their most damaging moments.

First, the cover-ups that were supposed to help left Melissa and Tracy vulnerable to the very things they most hoped to avoid, simply because they had concentrated on covering them up rather than immunizing themselves against them. But when each of them could see that her approach was not well received— in fact, that it wasn't working at all—she couldn't change tack.

Next, the "don't ask, don't tell" policy toward the peculiarity of the conversation itself condemned what each of them actually did say to the misinterpretations that constantly ran underneath their talk. One reason they stuck with "don't ask, don't tell" was that neither Melissa nor Tracy had a blueprint for speaking well in a tough moment. They couldn't find a neutral way to talk, and instead, they swung from one extreme to another.

On her side, Tracy saw two choices: stay on script, or blurt out what she really thought. She doggedly stayed on script as long as she could, even when the script sounded like an irrelevant rant. But by the end, Tracy was blurting out remarks that were much more damaging to her than losing her train of thought could ever be.

Melissa saw "sympathetic" and she saw "provoked," but she couldn't see middle ground between the two. She took Tracy's provocations on the chin as long as she could and then reacted with the heat she really felt. By the end of the conversation, a furious Melissa had swung from sympathy and softness to accusations. ("Confuse 'em or brutalize 'em," is the way one newspaper editor characterizes that swing.)

At those last, lowest moments, both cover-ups and "don't ask, don't tell" dropped away, but that's not the good news it should be, because they were replaced with the by-now-familiar damaging judgments. From the beginning, Melissa's softness had seemed fake to Tracy, but Melissa's final accusation struck her as authentic. From the beginning, Tracy's canned speeches had seemed fake to Melissa, but Tracy's blurted suspicions struck her as simultaneously ridiculous and characteristic. At this worst possible moment, both Melissa and Tracy were confirmed in their poor opinions of each other. "This is what I assumed she was like," each of them thought. "I was right; except, she's worse."

## Strategies for the unpredictable breakdowns

It is the nature of two-level, tough conversations—with communication up top, where it's observable, and interpretation with all its flaws concealed below—that we won't see breakdowns like Melissa and Tracy's coming. That doesn't mean, however, that we can't handle the conversations themselves. Parkour traceurs also know that unpredictable things can happen. Instead of being blindsided by the unexpected, traceurs face it with their customary "What have we got here?" attitude. For us, these hard-to-read conversations could be like parkour in the dark.

Traceurs are able to cross a landscape at night. There is a lot that they, like us, can't see, but their skills haven't changed. Their strategies for moving through a tough landscape in balance haven't abandoned them. They still know the tactics they have learned—the leaps, vaults, landings, and rolls—to surmount obstacles in their path.

In tough conversations, our first central principle, too, has been to stick to *skill*, whether the combat mentality brought issues of strategy to the fore or emotional loads brought issues of tactics to the fore. Good strategy gave us an alternative to conversational warfare. Good tactics gave us an alternative to emotional overloads. And now, when the likelihood of misconceptions is front and center, strategic and tactical issues come together as an alternative to conversation breakdowns.

We'll need to pull together everything we have, because nearly every tough conversation, like those between Melissa and Tracy—is layered. Combat, emotion, and misconceptions almost never show up one at a time. Together, they are almost fiendishly designed to push us off balance. But our second principle of good communication in tough conversations has been to stick to *balance*, like traceurs in a tricky landscape. So we will still openly respect ourselves, respect our counterparts, and respect the problems in the landscape of the conversation between us. The balance point we're looking for is where those three forms of respect come together; we still want to play out the conversation there. That's our job, and we can do it unilaterally.

To look first at the strategic side, we want a strategy that assumes we are likely to be taken by surprise. We want a strategy absolutely rooted in the fact that there is a great deal about this conversation that we don't know. We don't know how our counterpart sees things or will interpret us. We don't know how our counterpart is going to move, respond, or react. We want a strategy that is flexible enough to *allow* for differences between intentions and perceptions on both sides and that sets us up to move in response to what's going on in the moment—on our side and on our counterpart's side—without depending on our counterpart to do the same.

I call the strategies in this chapter "Mock Interview" and "Put myself in your shoes" and they come from—and build on—the change-the-game strategy in chapter 7. Mock Interview brings back three points of strategy that we've seen before:

- Preferred outcome ("Where do I want to get in this conversation?")

- Preferred working relationship ("How do I want this relationship to be?")

- Interferences ("What's interfering with the relationship I want?")

Mock Interview then adds two new perspectives on the problem between us, and points of strategy for those perspectives. This is reassuring, because it means we have or will get the skills for hard-to-read conversations, even layered ones. The biggest trick is putting those skills in play when so much pressure is on. We'll find help with that when we get to tactics later in the chapter.

The Mock Interview strategy prep gives you the raw material you need to go into a hard talk with a counterpart who is unlikely to see the situation the way you do. What would Mock Interview look like in practice?

## Strategy: The Mock Interview

The Mock Interview is an advance strategy: if you're planning to go into a difficult conversation, you hold your Mock Interview beforehand. You aren't, in fact, working with your counterpart, because he isn't there. But you are going to interview him as though he were there—right after you interview yourself. (Later, we'll look at how to do it on your feet.)

The first question in your Mock Interview, "What's the problem?" is one you ask yourself. You are the expert on this one. Here's the twist: when you ask what the problem is, you're not looking for the single right answer or the answer most favorable to your side. You're looking for multiple answers—you want to answer the question as broadly as you can. So every time you come up with an answer, ask the question again.

Why are you trying to come up with, say, eight answers when you're used to coming up with the single best one? Because you're going into a difficult conversation with someone who probably doesn't look at any problem the way you do, and you don't want to drive this conversation into the breakdown gap before you even meet with your counterpart. The more broadly you think about the problem, the likelier it is that you and your counterpart will overlap somewhere. That doesn't mean, however, that you're going to hold back the parts where the two of you are not on the same page.

For the second question—"How would my counterpart describe the problem?"—you can't literally ask about his side, because your counterpart is not there for your Mock Interview strategy prep. Nevertheless, most people are very good at imagining what a problem *might* look like to their counterpart, even if they don't like that viewpoint. Give it your best shot, or get a strategy buddy to help you. You'll handle this question the same way you did the first one: asking the question again every time you answer it and coming up with half a dozen or more answers even if they are completely unrelated and even if you disagree with them. Then add three more answers:

- "There is no problem." It's possible that you're taking your counterpart by surprise and that this is the first time the other person has heard about a problem. For example, Gil, the outgoing department head in chapter 10, didn't know Delia thought he had been attacking Mary's ideas, and when he did know, he didn't agree. "There is no problem" is also the answer usually given by someone who dismisses the problem or resists the conversation altogether.

- "*You* are the problem." More often than not, that's exactly what the counterpart thinks—not "we have a problem," but "it's you." Delia believed this about Gil.

- "I don't know how you see it." In fact, you don't know how your counterpart sees this, although you're doing your best to try to see it his way.

That last answer—"I don't know how you see it"—is more useful than it might look. It can be a good way to open, and we're always looking for how to get a conversation underway. If Melissa had said to Tracy very early on, "I've been thinking about how the pressure in the office on Drew looks to you, and I realize I *don't*

## Melissa's Mock Interview prep

### What's the problem?

Tracy unsettles Drew, and Drew finds it difficult to work around her.

I end up managing Drew, while Tracy should be managing her own assistant.

There's a problem of low morale in Tracy's office at a difficult time.

At a time when Drew needs to be highly efficient, his efficiency is reduced.

Tracy drives me nuts.

### What would my counterpart—Tracy—say the problem is?

Tracy would say:

There's too much work.

I can't do everything.

It isn't me.

*know*—I don't know how you see it," that would have been neither soft nor harsh. It would have been neutral, focused, and true.

For that matter, if Tracy had said to Melissa, "I've been thinking
about how you see the work situation in my office and I realize *I
don't know*," she in turn would have been neutral, focused, and honest. Nothing there would confuse her or make her back down.

That's a start, but what about the rest? What, specifically,
would the Mock Interview prep look like for Melissa and Tracy?
This is where we'll pick up from chapter 7 and add *preferred outcome*, *preferred working relationship*, and *interferences* to the two new
strategy questions to make a package deal. Melissa and Tracy would
want to write out their Mock Interview prep so that they could

There is no problem: Drew has never said anything to me.

Melissa is the problem.

I (Melissa) don't know how Tracy sees the problem.

### What's my preferred outcome?

Tracy minds her temper around Drew.

Drew's morale remains high.

### What's my preferred working relationship with Tracy?

Tracy keeps the financial house in order.

Tracy manages all that comes up, with support from Drew.

Tracy manages Drew without my direct involvement.

Tracy can see the big picture.

Tracy won't backtrack in conversation or drill down into minute
detail.

see what they have. They have done that here (see "Melissa's Mock Interview Prep" and "Tracy's Mock Interview Prep").

## From two sides now

The ability to plan good strategy isn't the kind of skill we want to be better at than everyone else. Melissa would *want* Tracy to plan strategy skillfully, and Tracy would want the same from Melissa.

Of course, strategy for a tough conversation can be much more aggressive or devious than the Mock Interview prep—anything can be distorted. When that happens, strategy itself becomes a thwarting ploy. For many people caught in the combat mentality, that's exactly what they use strategy for, although they may try to cover up. We don't want to abuse strategy on our side, because devious strategy is not in our interest and is hard on our reputation and relationships.

## Tracy's Mock Interview prep

### What's the problem?

The weight of the programs is on my shoulders.

I'm overstretched.

I have no work-life balance.

There's no proactive planning around the financial workload.

Melissa doesn't know what she's asking of me. She thinks complicated things are easy.

### What would my counterpart—Melissa—say the problem is?

Melissa would say:

If our counterpart uses a thwarting strategy, however, our own Mock Interview can serve as a neutralizing and disarming strategy in return, because it's nonreactive. It doesn't defer, it doesn't escalate, and it doesn't join in, so it doesn't push the conversation into breakdown. If we get sucked into the counterpart's ploys by mistake, then good strategy alone can pull us out. But we won't have strategy alone. We're going to combine it with tactics later in the chapter.

No matter what you come up with, there are three immediate benefits to the Mock Interview prep:

- The effort itself to think about both viewpoints sets up a conversation slanted toward clarifying views, not attacking or defending them. You won't, of course, insist on your version of the counterpart's view, but use it as a jumping-off place. And if, like Melissa and Tracy, you and your counterpart are on completely different tracks, you'll

There is no problem (because Melissa counts on me to stand between her and any problems).

Tracy is the problem.

I (Tracy) don't know how Melissa sees the problem.

**What's my preferred outcome?**

I want a better work-life balance.

I want better, proactive management of my workload.

**What's my preferred working relationship with Melissa?**

Melissa would have a keener awareness of the demands she makes on me.

find out fast. When the conversation goes live, if you can't or don't want to move onto the same track, you can stop the conversation and go back to the drawing board instead of getting caught up in guessing and interpreting a conversation that isn't making much sense.

- You can lower the emotional temperature. You're talking about a problem and how it looks to each of you, instead of reacting to each other. If your counterpart has not expected a strategy like this, has no idea what you're doing, and is suspicious—which happens—she is likely to attack, defend, or retreat. But to be successful, your counterpart's emotional tactics require a reaction from *you*, and you have something else to do besides react to what she does. What you say may indeed be met with thwarting ploys, but you're ready for that.

- Surprisingly, this kind of strategy is well received by a counterpart. You have thought about the conversation in advance—looking at both sides, rather than collecting ammunition for your side alone—and that brings a measure of respect and self-respect to the conversation that can help both of you.

Now that we have Mock Interviews for Melissa and Tracy, how do they use them?

## Changing strategy: Melissa

One of the main advantages of the Mock Interview is its flexibility. Once you bring your mind to bear on solving problems based on your own strategy, all kinds of ideas can occur to you.

If Melissa held her Mock Interview at arm's length, then simply with the information she provided unilaterally, *Melissa herself could see a link between Drew's problem with Tracy and Tracy's problem with feeling overworked.* Without even knowing that she and Tracy were coming at the conversation from different perspectives, Melissa could connect what concerned her with her own idea of Tracy's concerns. She could say, "Drew has told me that he's unsettled by the tension in your office, although he may not have mentioned it to you. He knows how much pressure you're under, and so do I." If Melissa started there, her opening would be focused, honest, and neutral. And Tracy would not react with the suspicion set off by Melissa's soft and off-topic original opening. In fact, Tracy would realize that Melissa does understand more than Tracy has given her credit for. Tracy might be defensive about her office management, but Melissa is *agreeing* that it's a problem, not *attacking* it as a problem.

Taking another tack, Melissa might look at her preferred working relationship, separate the wheat from the chaff, and *come up with a plan like the one she proposed in the first round to divide up the work between Tracy and Drew.* That was a good plan and one with which Tracy eventually agreed. This time, however, Melissa could more easily introduce the problem of Drew's morale, because his morale would be tied in with Tracy's own, not set against it.

Or Melissa might look at her preferred outcome and realize that it was *entirely dependent on Tracy.* It's never a good idea to leave the outcome you want in someone else's hands, so Melissa would be likely to rethink what she was trying to do. She might propose incentives to Tracy to get through the year-end with high morale in the office and make that proposal the opening focus of the conversation.

In fact, *Melissa might come up with something even better* than the starters here. As a side benefit to a good, flexible strategy, clashing styles won't affect her so much. With a robust strategy or two under way, she'll be busy enough with other lines of thought to take her mind off Tracy's annoying style.

But *what if Melissa couldn't pick out any intersection* between Tracy and her when she stood back and looked at her Mock Interview prep? Then a focused, honest, neutral opening akin to the one we considered earlier would be a natural place to start: "I've been thinking about how the tension between you and Drew in your office looks to you, and I realize I don't know. I don't know how you see it." Tracy might be surprised that Melissa mentioned Drew at all, but an opening focus on tension in her office will make sense to her. The conversation won't slip toward the breakdown gap at its first words.

## Changing strategy: Tracy

Back in the first round, Melissa's unexpected opening compliment confused Tracy and didn't fit with Tracy's idea of what the conversation was going to be about. Caught off guard, she fell back on her script. Because the conversation was on a track that Tracy hadn't anticipated, while her script was prepared for the conversation she *had* anticipated what she said didn't fit and, in fact, barely made sense. But because she and Melissa were following the "don't ask, don't tell" policy, neither of them stopped to unsnarl what was happening. Right there, at the first words from each of them, the conversation began sliding into the breakdown gap.

If instead Tracy had put into play the strategic idea that misreading people and mistaking their perspectives is a likely characteristic of difficult conversation, she might have taken another, much better tack when her red flag of suspicion and confusion went up at Melissa's soft opening.

"Okay, thank you, Melissa," Tracy could say in response to Melissa's compliment. She could go on, "*You've caught me off guard*, though, because when it's such a busy time and extra work has already come in, I think you want to talk to me about taking on even more. I think it's never going to stop."

This is exactly what's on her mind. The difference is that *she's talking in dialogue, not covering up her nerves with a script*. In this version, Tracy is using the blueprint for speaking well in a tough moment—clear content, neutral tone, temperate phrasing—to make a true, non-offensive point that comes out of her own Mock Interview prep. What has changed from her first, scripted version of the conversation is her strategy and her preparation. Now Tracy has real direction. She has used her own opening to respond to Melissa's, to make clear her own perspective on the conversation, and to launch her own concerns. With that, Tracy is *talking* to Melissa about managing the work, not *unloading* on her. Tracy herself is bringing respect and self-respect to an important and difficult conversation with her boss.

But *what if Tracy is wrong?* What if she picks out of her own Mock Interview prep something that's completely off base from Melissa's standpoint? The clear possibility is that Tracy would pick the thread that runs through all her prep: Melissa is oblivious to how hard Tracy's work is and how overburdened Tracy is—and Melissa doesn't want to know.

If she used the blueprint for speaking well, Tracy could *open with her reservations* about Melissa's awareness of her workload. She might say, "I feel as if the weight of the programs is on my shoulders, and I take the responsibility seriously. I want the machinery of the programs to run smoothly, and because it usually does, no one sees the furious paddling I'm doing underneath. But I'm badly overstretched now, and I don't think you see it."

Good point; well said; not right. Melissa does know what goes on in her department.

Even with a good-faith effort to see a problem from someone else's perspective, *you're going to get it wrong sometimes*. But even if you are wrong, the effort to see a problem from your counterpart's point of view is a nice switch from the combat mentality (see "Good Strategy for Gil and Delia"). Indeed it's so disarming that, instead of pitting their perspectives against yours, your counterparts will often try to correct your misimpression about their own perspectives. People want to feel understood when they aren't feeling defensive. Melissa would probably amend Tracy's misperception, telling Tracy that she does know, and wants to help.

## Good strategy for Gil and Delia

The habit of good strategy is not a sometime thing and is not just for special cases.

It can work for Gil, too. As described in chapter 10, the outgoing social studies department chair was dumbfounded when Delia accused him of attacking their colleague Mary's ideas. If he had the habit of strategy instead of reaction, Gil could say, right in the moment, either to himself or outright, "What has broken down here?"

And he could go on to say to Delia, "Attack Mary? Tell me: what did you hear that sounded like an attack from me? What did Mary hear?" He doesn't want to presume Delia's perspective, but he does want to recognize that she has one, and bring it up into the light.

If Gil uses the blueprint for speaking well in a tough moment, he can respect Delia's perspective without agreeing to it. He can bring self-respect to his own perspective without sounding defensive. Again, it's the habit of flexible strategy that would let him move to dialogue with Delia. If Gil simply reacts, defensiveness is likelier than dialogue. Does that mean it's not a difficult conversation anymore? No. But it's not toxic and won't have toxic fallout.

Gil had also been stung by Delia's frosty threat to his position at school in response to Gil's own offer of support. It would not be surprising if he were too triggered, too vulnerable, or simply too surprised to respond in the moment, or if he decided not to respond at all. We need a strategy that doesn't have a short expiration date. Any time—now, tomorrow, next week—Gil could use a Mock Interview opening to say to Delia, "I've been thinking about how it looked to you when I gave you notes on the doings of our department before the schools merged, and I realize that I don't know how you saw it."

What happened to Melissa's own preferred outcome ("Where do I want to get in this conversation?") concerning Drew's morale? Does she have to give that up to meet Tracy on her ground? No. We've already seen that *the two outcomes can fold in together*, and Melissa is capable of making it happen. With Tracy's opening and Melissa's response, the conversation that has two distinct perspectives on a problem has moved back from the brink of breakdown.

If they are tired of Mock Interview openings, Melissa or Tracy or Gil could go to Plan B and design a good "Put myself in your shoes" opening instead. They will find their own words in either case. But what's "Put myself in your shoes"?

## Plan B: Put myself in your shoes

All of us want a fallback approach to something as tricky as a tough conversation, if only because we already know it's better to have more than one thing to try. A second approach in your pocket gives you that much more flexibility, and one plan might work better in a particular moment than another. After Mock Interview, "Put myself in your shoes" is your fallback.

Let's look at Omar, the actor-manager of a theater program. Omar wants a second approach to a difficult conversation because he's angry with his counterpart, so nearly everything he came up with in his Mock Interview was negative.

### The theater manager and the voice coach

Omar, the head of the theater program, had hired a well-known coach, Duncan, to give singing lessons to the program's young actors. With considerable experience as a vocal coach himself, Omar had soon come to believe that Duncan's techniques were a risk to the students' voices in the long term. Duncan, on his side, had complete confidence in himself and his approach and wouldn't consider a change. Conversations about their disagreement had been testy, and Omar would not be renewing Duncan's contract.

Much as he wanted to avoid it, Omar would have to have a conversation with Duncan about the termination. The theater community was small, and the two of them couldn't help but run into each other again. But Duncan had been condescending to Omar, and Omar had resented it. "When I try to plan out what to say," Omar said, "I keep bringing up everything he said or did that got on my nerves. I know I should make 'I' statements and not 'you' statements, but either way, they all sound negative and personal. The whole conversation could end up being a mudslinging contest, because he'll come right back at me if I throw anything at him. In my darker moments, I know I would relish that, but I have two reputations to think of—mine and this program's. I've got to come up with something better."

Specifically because he was angry, Omar first wanted a strategic step that would help him disarm both himself and a tense conversation with Duncan, who was also angry. Second, Omar wanted strategic help to preserve—as much as he could—respect, reputation, and at least a minimally viable relationship between them. And third, he wanted to be able to keep his focus in the conversation and not follow suit if Duncan jumped in with name-calling or another thwarting ploy.

At the same time, Omar realized that if Duncan couldn't save face when he learned that his contract wouldn't be renewed, the coach might take the "if I can't win, no one's gonna win" approach, with damage all around. Omar wanted a strategy ready for that disconcerting possibility, too.

### Omar's "put myself in your shoes" opening

Plan B is a different way of working the strategic raw material that is the foundation of the Mock Interview strategy. If you're using "in your shoes" as your Plan B, then strategy begins with your answers to the Mock Interview question "How would my counterpart describe the problem?" For example, when Omar took Duncan's view of the problem between them, Omar came up with good information coated in incendiary language (see "Omar's Plan B").

When Omar tempered the language according to the blueprint for speaking well in a tough moment, he came up with this: "Duncan thinks I look over his shoulder and criticize what he does, even though I hired him for his expertise." Why did he change the language in his own strategy prep? People react to provocative phrasing, regardless of the content it is supposed to convey. Omar wanted to give his assessment of Duncan's likely point of view cool consideration, and temperate phrasing helps. As a side benefit, you can often come up with good phrasing for the conversation itself in the process. (Write it down, or you'll forget it immediately.)

Now, for an opening, "in your shoes" works this way: Omar will ask Duncan if he, Omar, understands Duncan's point of view on their problem. Omar might say, "Duncan, when I look at the

## Omar's plan B

### What would my counterpart—Duncan—say the problem is?

Duncan would say:

Omar interferes with me when I do the work he hired me to do.

I don't have the autonomy I expected.

Omar likes what I do one day and criticizes me the next.

Omar treats me like a quack.

In this company, you don't get your due as an expert.

Omar disrespects me and the years I've put into this.

He's trying to ruin my reputation.

last four months from your point of view, it seems like I'm looking over your shoulder and don't give you room to work with your own techniques."

This is a good start to a conversation about ending a contract that is going to take place between an angry manager and an angry coach because it breaks a pattern that counterparts have learned to resist: our tendency to go into a difficult conversation like Omar's and explain our side. Of course, explaining our own side encourages our counterpart to push back by explaining his side. Even if it isn't what we're aiming for, the consequences are that both sides harden into the positions they just explained. (Some people gamely try to avoid this outcome by asking the other side to go first, but the consequences are the same.)

Omar felt better with a good opening, and he decided to press on. Going back to his Mock Interview prep, Omar's preferred working relationship and preferred outcome were clear to him: he wanted to end his working relationship with Duncan and was in a position to do so. However, Omar also wanted an adequately collegial connection between the two of them—better than they had at the moment—so they wouldn't have a gossip-worthy feud going on in the theater world. (Why not aim higher? Why not shoot for happiness on both sides? If Omar sets Duncan's happiness as his own goal, Omar can easily fail to gain his own preferred outcome if Duncan is not fully satisfied with the non-renewal of his contract. And realistically, Duncan *is* likely to be unhappy with that. Omar doesn't want to set for his preferred outcome a bar so high that he can't get over it himself. Although it is a tremendous outcome if you can get it, mutual happiness as a preferred outcome in difficult conversations is a quick route to hypernice behavior and giving in on the one hand or bailing out on the other.)

The desire to preserve a collegial connection with Duncan gave Omar a problem, because he and Duncan had already done some damage with the angry and offensive sniping that had been going back and forth up until now. Omar wanted to change tack, but he needed more help with the conversation itself, more protection from his own tendency to go negative.

When you're preparing your strategy, you don't want to sidestep what you actually think and feel. Since your counterpart will never see this prep, go ahead and shine a light on your own least-constructive thoughts and feelings now—so they are less likely to leak out from under a cover-up later.

With that in mind, Omar spilled his reactions freely in his Mock Interview prep. And he got past the vitriol that had spewed onto paper when he answered the questions "What's the problem?" and "What would my counterpart—Duncan—say the problem is?" That's how Omar realized that there was indeed something on the two lists that overlapped: both he and Duncan believed strongly in their work, even though they didn't agree on how it should be done.

"I could make a conversation out of that," Omar said. "Putting aside all the personal stuff, we really do have a basic philosophical disagreement about developing a singing voice. That's the real problem. I don't have to make 'I' statements or 'you' statements. I can make 'philosophy' statements. I can admit Duncan's experience and his concepts, but not agree to allow them in practice here. That's a valid disagreement; we can both take the high road, and personal slams don't have to come into it. I like it."

With "philosophy" at the heart of his side of the conversation, Omar could prepare for a conversation that was more objective and less subjective, which was what he wanted.

## Strategic change

In the course of thinking about strategy, Omar's whole idea about talking to Duncan had changed. The difference was not that Omar had come up with one foolproof strategic option, but that he simply felt willing to go back into communication with Duncan—a move that until recently he had been completely avoiding. A tough conversation looks different to him now, and that's a lot of the advantage of having good strategy. It's not so much one particular thing you decide to do, but the feeling that the game has changed.

The Mock Interview strategy gives us a good place to stand when we can't see what's happening, our counterpart can't either,

## "Put myself in your shoes"

### Melissa

If Melissa wanted an "in your shoes" opening, she would do what Omar had done and take her material from her Mock Interview prep and then temper the language. She might say to Tracy, "Drew has told me that the tension in your office is affecting him. If I were in your shoes, I would feel as though there isn't enough time to do the work and simultaneously give more management attention to Drew. That would just be one more demand on you. It must seem to you that your own morale is in jeopardy because of this double-tasking you have to do now, and so it makes sense that Drew feels it, too. It would look like there's nothing personally amiss between you and Drew; it's how things are going in your office. Am I right, here? Is that how it looks to you?"

### Tracy

And if Tracy, using her Mock Interview prep, wanted to start with "in your shoes," she might say, "If I were in your shoes, Melissa, I would feel like you could ask anything of me. You would think that my capacity for work is very elastic. You would know that Fisk hadn't planned to have his numbers crisis right at year-end. I think your attention would really be on having this work out for Fisk. Do I correctly understand how it looks to you? If I do, that gives us our problem."

and we're both inclined to guess about what we don't know. "In your shoes" gives us a good fallback opening to Mock Interview, if we want it.

Looking back at Melissa and Tracy's conversation, it's clear that good strategy could solve a lot of the medium-sized problems between them. But in a conversation as out of balance as theirs was—with one counterpart as nervous and confused as Tracy, and the other as angry and insulted as Melissa—thwarting ploys can be severe. And because strategy is behind the scenes while thwarting ploys are in their faces, it's the ploys that people worry about most. In fact, that's what most people think of when they think about tough conversations. What are we going to do about the worst thwarting ploys that come up?

## Tactics for thwarting ploys

You'll recognize some, if not all, of these next types of examples. Taken together, they show how widely spaced thwarting ploys can be on the intention span. They range from the completely unconscious end to the flat-out malevolent end. The problem is that we can't be sure which is which, even if we think we know.

As we saw in chapter 8, when thwarting ploys are intentional, their function rarely changes: people who use them are trying to get you to back off where they are vulnerable. But is there a way to tell when someone is using a thwarting ploy intentionally? The truth is we can't know for sure; that's information we just don't have. We can ask, but a counterpart using high-caliber thwarting ploys is probably also playing her cards very close to the vest. We can guess, but that's a gambler's stand. As we saw in the box "Complications in the Breakdown Gap," in chapter 10, no one has direct access to his counterpart's intentions.

The better question is this: are we vulnerable to the ploy? And if we are, can we respond well to it, as opposed to play into it or just reflexively react to it?

If we want to handle thwarting ploys better, we cannot use tactics that depend on knowing our counterparts' intentions. Instead, we need something that will work at any point on the intention span—anywhere we're vulnerable. We're looking for all-purpose tactics. With that in mind, wherever we think our counterpart is on the intention span, we will start at middle ground.

## What to do

In a difficult conversation, no matter how we read our counterpart's ploy, and no matter what we think her intention is, we want to make our first response as though she's *innocently offensive*.

### Innocent offense

Austin was a junior technology manager who had mixed feelings about speaking up to his senior manager, Oksana, who often shouted at him. On the one hand, Oksana was one-up; on the other, being shouted at was disturbing. Using the blueprint for speaking well in a tough moment, Austin came up with words he could live with: "I can hear your points better at lower volume." He felt better having a comment he could use if he did decide to speak up.

Late that afternoon, Austin listened to his messages and one was from Oksana. He was glad it was late because he could leave the information she wanted without talking to her. But when he called, unfortunately, Oksana answered. Soon she was yelling at him over the phone. So Austin said to her, "I can hear your points better at lower volume." The line was briefly silent, and then Oksana hung up on him. Austin sat holding the phone, shaken.

The next moment, Oksana was standing in Austin's doorway. "Is that it?" she asked. "Is that why people don't talk to me?"

That was a very surprising outcome to Austin. He had believed Oksana shouted intentionally, because she was used to having the upper hand and because she got away with it. In fact, however, Oksana was "innocently offensive." Yes, her shouting troubled other people, but she didn't shout *intending* to trouble them—she wasn't aware that she shouted at all. Regardless of how Austin and others perceived her behavior, her shouting was off her radar and its consequences were unintended, although the consequences to her reputation and relationships were themselves troubling.

There are advantages to assuming that our counterpart is innocently offensive:

- Like Oksana, our counterparts are often actually unaware of a problem. They'll stop what they're doing because they didn't intend anything by it to begin with. They may need reminding, if the ploy is unconscious, but they'll stop.

- By beginning with a neutral response, we won't escalate the problem between us. We've seen again and again that when we react to what we think are thwarting ploys, we usually overreact. Our counterpart takes a big reaction from our side as a thwarting ploy itself, and the conversation slides into the breakdown gap. If Austin had said to Oksana, "You always shout at me and it's not right," his response would not be neutral, even though to him it's true. The remark would sound aggressive to an unsuspecting Oksana, and she'd respond from there.

- Third, we don't have to guess right. Is our counterpart innocently offensive or using a thwarting ploy? We don't need to know. The neutral response will serve us well in both cases.

Really? In some cases, innocent offense is a very generous assumption. In the next example, Sam had no idea what was going on with his counterpart, Jessica, but he was sure that she was not innocently offensive. In fact, she was all over the place—distorting his words, accusing him, even threatening him. If Jessica meant to thwart Sam, and all he did was make a neutral comment, wouldn't

Jessica score off him? That's a credible concern, but something might influence us to choose a neutral response even if we think our counterpart is intentionally using a thwarting ploy, and that is the *threshold of aggression*.

### Threshold of aggression

Jessica, a senior manager at an IT firm, was leading a presentation to a client, and the information was weak and disorganized. The client had been patient, then quiet, then clearly exasperated. When the presentation really started to fall apart, the client put the team on the spot with questions that made them look increasingly inadequate.

On this particular day, Sam, also a senior manager at the IT firm, had not been part of the presenting team; he was simply observing, and he was as surprised at Jessica's poor performance as the client had been. After the client left, he asked Jessica, "What happened?"

Jessica immediately took offense. Angry and red in the face, she barked at Sam, "You're not my boss, so don't start patronizing me. You always undercut me, no matter what I do."

Sam recoiled. He replayed in his mind what had just happened, but couldn't figure out what had provoked Jessica. So he tried to smooth things over. "Sorry, Jessie," he said. "It must have been a tough morning."

But Jessica continued to lash out at Sam, her antagonism palpable. Each time he spoke, she interrupted him with accusations and threats, eventually saying, "I can't wait to see how you like it when you're hung out to dry."

Sam tried to stay reasonable, but Jessica didn't wind down. Getting more directive, he said, "Pull yourself together. You're twisting every word I say."

But nothing changed.

Unquestionably, to Sam, Jessica's tirade following the presentation debacle did *not* look like innocent offense. Afterward, Sam said, "Jessica and I had worked together pretty well for a long time. We were under pressure of time to fix the mess with the client, so I couldn't just wait until she decided to pull herself together. I'd known her to come down pretty hard on people who weren't performing; in fact, I used to agree with her point, if not her method. But this was outrageous. It was a complete distortion. I couldn't talk with someone who twisted what happened and what I said."

And so he didn't talk to her, which cost him dearly. Both were passed over for promotion after the company pinned the loss of the client directly on their persistent failure to communicate.

Jessica's distortions and threats worked for her as thwarting ploys are meant to: they got Sam to back off. The bungled presentation was a very raw and touchy subject, and Sam was no longer asking her about it.

Nevertheless, Jessica might have moved away from her own ploys, because people have definite levels of aggression that they're comfortable with—and they are reluctant to step up from there. Our threshold of aggression and our counterpart's may not be the same, but we each have one. In a difficult conversation, if we "talk to the ploy" neutrally it may surprise us when that alone puts our counterpart over her threshold of aggression and she steps back herself. Sam might not be able to stop Jessica's tirade, but she might stop herself.

There are many ways to shift what feels right to the counterpart away from aggression. What these tactics have in common is that they neutralize thwarting ploys. It's worth noting here that while thwarting ploys come in clusters, we handle them one at a time. Dealing well with the first face-off doesn't mean there won't be another. Especially when we can't read our counterpart's intention—or perhaps especially when we think we can—starting at neutral can take some changing on our side. Sam could add as many of these as he wanted to his stock of tactics and draw on them when he needed to:

- Sam would "talk to the ploy" if he said to Jessica during their conversation what he said about it later: "We've worked together pretty well for a long time. I don't know how to talk about what went wrong in the presentation when your take on what happened, and what's going on now, is so different from mine."

- He could change the sudden confrontation into a point of agreement. When Jessica said, "You're not my boss, so don't start patronizing me. You always undercut me, no matter what I do," Sam doesn't have to push back or back down. He could respect her take on the conversation, even if it's a stretch. "I see how you took what I said the way you did," he might say. "That wasn't what I meant. Let me try again." Sam would simply disarm Jessica's shot, unilaterally. If her twist was a hostile thwarting ploy, Sam would not concur to appease her. (When Sam remembered the conversation, saying "sorry" was the remark he regretted most. Given the outcome, it still made him angry.) Instead, he would accept and retry. No one would score off the other, and no one would be drawn off topic.

- Sam might go to middle ground between Jessica's view and his own by combining both to make a new starting point: "Whoa, Jessica, I'm not the enemy. I'm on your side." That's a different way for Sam to be reasonable. Yes, Jessica's conduct was overblown, but it wasn't incomprehensible, given the agonizing loss of face she had just suffered in the presentation. With a simple response like that, Sam could reach a hand across the breakdown gap without getting squishy. What happened to his anger at her distortions? Nothing. It's still there, but Sam is responding from skill, not gut reaction. Being reasonable is not foreign to him; he's just changing how he handles himself in a tough conversation.

In any of these cases, if she responded to Sam's tactic by using the same thwarting ploy again, Jessica might put herself over her own threshold of aggression. In the first case, it is simply harder for our counterpart to use the same ploy a second time if she has to own it because we called it—clearly, neutrally, and temperately. In the second case, we are a pointless target of aggression if we grant our counterpart her perception and try unwaveringly to make ourselves clear. And in the third case, it's harder for her to justify her ploy when we step aside from the ploy with respect and self-respect. None of these is a forceful response and none is intended to be. They are neutral.

But Sam had not blown a client presentation or attacked Jessica himself, so he had the moral high ground in the confrontation. If Jessica provoked him without cause, why not provoke her back? Because Sam didn't want to be a reaction machine. He didn't want to teach Jessica that she can wind him up and get a big reaction any more than he wanted to teach her that when she escalates, he will back off. Sam had his eye on who he wants to be.

### Good intentions are not enough

Lydia, an expert researcher, was a mature, small, soft-spoken woman, and the senior analyst in her office. When she was presenting her findings to clients, she often found that her colleagues, Nick and Parvati, stepped in and took over for her.

Although it offended her, she knew without question that they meant well, and she didn't confront them with her resentment. "We have a very good working relationship," Lydia said, "and I don't want to create tension that would spoil it." This pattern has been going on for two years, though, and Lydia was looking for a change—if she could get it without spoiling the relationship.

Whereas Sam was trying to straighten out his tough conversation with Jessica, after two years Lydia hadn't even gotten hers started. She was convinced that Nick and Parvati were innocently offensive, but her conviction hadn't been an advantage to her. In fact, because she knew they meant well, in her mind, anything she said would look as if she were overreacting to how the presentations were handled. She would look like a spoiler, she thought. So to Lydia, talking about the problem looked worse than having the problem, and she said nothing.

There were other reasons why Lydia thought a conversation with Nick and Parvati about their tendency to step in for her during presentations fit into the "I can't go there" type of difficult conversation. Hypernice by habit, Lydia weighed Nick and Parvati's good intentions more heavily than she weighed their regrettable "rescues" during presentations, even though the rescues were a long-standing frustration. Also, because Lydia had a very low threshold of aggression, she saw no difference between a conversation about a problem and a straight-out confrontation.

And Lydia had one last worry. She was sure that if she mentioned that she didn't want to be rescued in presentations, Nick and Parvati would protest that they meant well. Because she agreed with them, she worried that she would back away from her own point of view and defer to theirs. Then she'd have the worst of both worlds—she would create tension, they would still step in for her during presentations, and she would still resent it. No wonder she avoided the conversation. It was as though being aware of what can go wrong in the breakdown gap were a handicap.

Nevertheless, Lydia worked to put together strategy and tactics to speak to Nick and Parvati. And one afternoon, she said to them, "Remember our last presentation to the client, when I was talking about my research and you chimed in? When you did, I knew you meant to back me up. I felt like I faded back, though, and when that happens, I feel diminished."

As she thought they would, Nick and Parvati immediately protested that in every presentation, hers was the best and most important research; that they didn't mean to steal the stage (and they couldn't anyway, not next to her); and that, yes, they were just backing her up. Lydia listened and nodded her understanding. When they stopped, she said again, "I feel diminished when I fade back." And this time, Nick and Parvati listened and nodded that they understood.

If we have said what we have to say while using the blueprint for speaking well in a tough moment, and our point is clear, neutral, and temperate, then repetition is not a mistake. In Lydia's case, *staying* with her point was even more of a concern to her than *making* her point. The more we jump around with what we say, the more we open the door to different readings by our counterparts. When our words are a good fit, we want to keep them.

To keep difficult conversations from breaking down, we need good strategy and good tactics to back up our good intentions. We don't want to have to guess what the right thing to do is when we can't read our counterparts and when we don't know how they are reading us. And we don't want to try to decide whether to escalate or back down, whether to cover up our reactions or blurt them out, whether to follow our counterpart's track or insist on our own—or whether to avoid the conversation altogether.

The strategies for difficult conversations in this chapter don't set us up to ignore what's going on with our counterparts, but they do not hinge on what they are doing on their side, either. Instead, these strategies help us improve our toughest conversations unilaterally. They let us line up our intentions with our words, and they give us forward motion of our own that doesn't come at our counterpart's expense.

The tactics in this chapter help us find a way to say what we have to say that is clear and effective—not soft or harsh, but starting from middle ground every time. We will be speaking closer to reality than is often the case in difficult conversations, and we will want to use our own voice. Using the blueprint for speaking well in tough moments, I have come up with words for the people in the examples here to illustrate strategy and tactics for them to use, but those aren't words we need to use. In fact, there's no one right thing to say in any of these conversations. If there were, it would immediately become a cliché and lose its effectiveness.

There's always the worry that we'll be blindsided by a difficult conversation and won't have time to prepare an elaborate strategy or come up with the perfect phrase. Fortunately, however, good strategy and technique become second nature, in part because they are based on our own vulnerabilities, and we know what those are. Although there are many variables in the people, the topics, and the tactics involved, our vulnerabilities remain quite steady. If a trigger has come up for us before, we can safely assume it will come up again, and between times, when we're calm, we can work on strategy and tactics to carry us over the bumps in our own road.

In the next chapter, we'll apply what we've put together to an example we've seen before. Let's see how we can pull a bad conversation out of breakdown and help Mike and Jack from chapter 1 salvage their relationship, if that's possible.

## Remember:

- To stop the slide into the breakdown gap, we want a good, balanced strategy that is flexible enough to allow for differences between intentions and perceptions on both sides, and that assumes we will be taken by surprise.

- The *Mock Interview* strategy prep gives both sides good material to take into a tough conversation with a counterpart who probably doesn't see the situation the way we do.

- *Plan B: Put myself in your shoes* extends our range—
  the more strategy preps we have, the better.

- *Innocent offensiveness*, *threshold of aggression*, and *good
  intentions are not enough* show how widely spaced
  thwarting ploys can be on the intentions span. They
  give us all-purpose tactics to use where we are vulnerable, regardless of our counterpart's intentions.

## CHAPTER 12

# Conclusion

## *Getting Back on Track*

W HILE THE PARTICULAR combinations of people, problems, and situations that complicated the difficult conversations in this book made each one different from the others, the ways those conversations broke down are beginning to fall into recognizable patterns of combat mentality, emotional reaction, and misconceptions. Until now, the big patterns that have derailed conversations over and over again have also been the hardest for us to deal with. But the old problems now have new solutions.

Let's look back at Jack and Mike from chapter 1, two friends who wanted to turn a company around and who eventually found themselves in a conversation so damaging that it makes you want to cover your eyes. Let's see if it's clearer now what was breaking down in their conversation and what they could do to handle it well.

# Jack and Mike: The company turnaround

You may remember that Jack, the CEO of his family's company, had brought his old friend Mike in as senior vice president to help him rev up the business. Mike wasn't sure how to react when managers pushed back against the slew of changes. Through the grapevine, Jack heard that Mike was heavy-handed and he could see that Mike was creating as many problems as he solved. But Jack said nothing.

Things came to a head in a senior managers meeting. Gus, an experienced manager, first offered Jack his resignation and then led the other managers in harsh criticism of Mike's performance. Mike, humiliated and distraught, looked to Jack for support. But instead of giving it to him, Jack as much as asked if Mike himself wanted to resign. Later, when Jack and Mike were alone, the two longtime friends attacked each other with accusations and threats. Mike did not resign. The expense and fallout from the litigation necessary to fire him would have been destructive to both men and to the company.

Like many other difficult conversations, this one broke down a little more every step of the way. Jack and Mike were out of balance from the first rumblings of dissatisfaction right through their final confrontation. Yet, from what we've seen in previous chapters, we can start to pick out and tag what happened between them. There's a lot that's familiar, and because we're looking in from the outside, we can see some of it before Jack and Mike hit their ultimate confrontation.

### Misconceptions

In this case, there were no bad intentions on either side. From the beginning, however, there were misconceptions. Jack and Mike had conflicting views of their working relationship—but they didn't know it. Jack, who thought he was helping Mike out by taking him on board, knew that Mike's manner with employees was abrasive—but didn't talk to Mike about it. And Mike, who thought he was carrying the ball for Jack through some tough opposition, couldn't figure out why Jack wasn't supporting him when managers resisted—but didn't ask. "Don't ask, don't tell" is a familiar early step in the chain reaction to breakdown. Why didn't Jack and Mike check in with each other? They didn't say anything, unfortunately, *because* they genuinely liked each other.

Not wanting to jeopardize their friendship, Jack and Mike were also covering up. On his side, Jack was covering up his anger and annoyance at Mike's missteps, although sometimes his irritation leaked out. When it did, Jack swung from hypernice (an affectionate arm across Mike's shoulders) to offensive (losing his temper with Mike or making jokes at his expense) in a way that was hard to read. Meanwhile, Mike on his side was covering up not only his uncertainty about how to handle the managers who were pushing back, but also his uneasiness that Jack wasn't backing him up. Cover-ups like these are a second familiar step toward breakdown.

Much more damage, however, was done in the last two steps in the chain reaction to breakdown, both of which Jack and Mike took. In the third step, when tension between them reached fever pitch, both sides dropped the cover-up and let their pent-up feelings rip. Finally, at the rawest moment, each counterpart took the fourth step—severely judging the other. With that, the breakdown was complete. In the end, of course, Jack and Mike didn't just jeopardize their friendship; they probably lost it.

### Emotional overload

Big emotions—anger, embarrassment, and fear—came into play here, too. Jack was initially annoyed by Mike's ham-handedness, but he was also uncomfortable and anxious about starting a conversation with him. Eventually, however, having bottled up his anger for too long, Jack was ripe for confrontation after Gus's diatribe. On his side, Mike was angry about his public dressing-down, thoroughly humiliated when Jack hung him out to dry, and apprehensive about the consequences of failure.

By the end of the afternoon, Jack and Mike had both fallen into the worst possible emotional behaviors, which felt justified to each of them because of the other's behavior. Mike attacked Jack and accused him of betrayal. Not to be outdone by his friend, Jack attacked and accused Mike back, and then raised the stakes by threatening him. At that point, it was impossible for either of them to find a neutral way to talk. And neither man could find a way to recover from the other's slams or from his own actions. True to form for anyone in the grip of big emotions, first Mike and then Jack slid into the combat mentality.

### Combat mentality

At the height of the confrontation set up by Gus and the other managers, both Jack and Mike saw a zero-sum battle—Gus would win or Mike would, but not both. What would determine the outcome of the battle? The CEO's power. Jack would take a stand with one side and abandon the other. As we saw, Jack backed Gus and the managers, with devastating consequences for Mike, for their friendship, and, in due course, for the company.

Almost everything Jack or Mike did or didn't do in this mess made their situation worse. But this conversation did not have to go on—or end—as it did. Jack and Mike did not use (because they didn't have them) the crucial elements that would have brought balance to their conversations and to their relationship: good strategy, effective tactics, and three-way respect. In fact, compared to what Jack and Mike put themselves and the company through, good strategy and effective tactics are simple.

## What to do: Strategy

It's no one's first choice to plan strategy while in crisis mode. But whether we're planning in our own good time or we're on the spot, the basics of good strategy for a tough conversation don't change: balance and three-way respect.

Gus was the only player here with a strategy, and certainly, he meant to put his CEO, Jack, on the spot. But Jack didn't have to play into that ploy; he could get time to think. He could have handed back Gus's resignation and said, "This is unexpected. I want to think about what you've said, not answer you off the cuff. I won't accept your resignation now. I'd like the two of us to talk first thing in the morning. And Mike, can we talk at the end of the day today?" Then, using Mock Interview questions, Jack could begin planning strategy for his first conversation, the one with Mike (see "Jack's Mock Interview Prep").

### Preferred outcome

Just by asking himself, "What's my preferred outcome in this conversation with Mike?" Jack would swap the habits of combat, emotional reaction, and misconceptions for strategic thinking. And given how the situation has gone so far, he is likely to be glad to drop those negatives. Jack might come up with a simple, genuine *preferred outcome* like this: "I want the two of us to look at our situation together and see it as a solvable problem."

In that moment, the problem is no longer simply Mike. Jack has put the problem in the landscape of the conversation, between the two of them. That slant on the conversation takes the onus off Mike and off Jack himself. It lets both of them look hard at the problem without requiring them to decide who's the villain and who's the victim. It simply goes at the problem from a different direction, not from the awkward confrontational tack Jack had been avoiding and then succumbed to. It gets them to the conversation they need to have.

A preferred outcome, even the CEO's preferred outcome, is never an assured outcome. There is a real possibility that Mike will come to the conversation with a very different tack and different outcome in mind—he might be in full combat mode, both defensive and offensive. But Jack is on good ground here.

## Jack's Mock Interview prep

### What's my preferred outcome?

I want the two of us to look at our situation together and see it as a solvable problem.

### What's my preferred working relationship with Mike?

Mike acts as a sounding board.

I make clearer than it has been which decisions are mine to make, so that Mike won't think he has to shoulder responsibility for doing more than he can do well.

Mike is clear about a better manner to use with others in the company.

Mike and I straighten out our priorities—Do change timetables take precedence over in-house relationships, or is it the other way around?

Mike thinks about and chooses his areas of strength and gets any professional development that he wants and might not have had as a lawyer. He thinks about new areas that he wants to take on and then develops his strengths there.

### What's interfering with my preferred working relationship with Mike?

We don't have a good feedback loop.

We have been unclear about decision-making limits.

Mike is unaware of how he is perceived by other managers.

The scope of Mike's work is probably unmanageably broad now.

And a preferred outcome like Jack's will automatically lead the conversation to preferred working relationship and interference, which we've seen is a useful way to look at a thorny problem in a precarious relationship.

There is also some possibility that Jack might have reached the point where his preferred outcome is "I want Mike to leave the company." In that case, Jack's strategy starts with a call to his lawyer. They need to look over Mike's contract and, given what's in the contract, begin finding incentives for Mike to leave. Then Jack's conversation with Mike would revolve around the incentives and the exit.

If Jack decides that his preferred outcome is "I want Mike to leave the company and we will still be friends," he may find the outcome much more difficult to get. If he still wants to try, Jack's strategy planning will be more complex, but not fundamentally different.

### Preferred relationship with interferences

When Jack takes the next strategy step, putting his *preferred working relationship* into words for himself, the first thing he will see is that he has to look at two different relationships with Mike— his preferred relationship with a close friend and his preferred working relationship with a colleague. Simply by framing his strategy this way, Jack makes it possible, in a way it hasn't been before, to discuss both with Mike.

Looking just at the second side of their relationship, that of CEO and senior vice president, four or five characteristics might come up, a couple from their situation so far and a couple from the preferred-outcome step above.

Side by side with that list, Jack could look openly at *interferences* with the working relationship he wants to have with Mike. From here, Jack can take a satellite view of the conversation and move it in any number of directions to look at a "solvable problem" between two men who are both friends and colleagues. With a parkour traceur's "What have we got here?" attitude, Jack could tell Mike what he himself thinks about what has been happening. Or he could ask Mike how the situation looks to him, or both men could start working out together how to make the dual relationship work better.

This conversation does not need to come to an embarrassing and angering series of criticisms, even though problems and what to do about them are a significant part of the conversation. There are many, many things that the two of them, and particularly Mike himself, can do to put Mike in a better position to work with the company's managers.

Unilaterally, Jack can come up with a Mock Interview strategy like this for a conversation with Mike. He is not dependent on anyone's sharing his intention, his perspective, his desire, or his skill. In fact, he can use the same strategy to prepare for his follow-up conversation with Gus.

And Mike himself can do a comparable strategy (see "Strategy for Mike").

If Jack and Mike do get as far as a one-on-one conversation after the managers' meeting—if they don't give in to the combat mentality and if they rate strategy ahead of emotional reactions for now—the two of them together could follow the same steps to prepare strategy for a second meeting with the senior managers. They could take the next Mock Interview steps, working up "What's our problem?" from their own point of view and "How would my counterpart describe the problem?" from the managers' point of view. Jack has heard a lot of talk through the grapevine, and both he and Mike heard enough in those difficult forty-five minutes in the last meeting to know what problems the managers see. If Jack and Mike combined the managers' perspectives and their own, they would find three major problems: first, the tension between the desire for change and the pain of change; second, how to balance the two; and third, the poor experience most of them have had so far. Jack and Mike could then put those problems in the landscape of a new conversation for *all* of them—executives and managers alike—to discuss.

## Strategy for Mike

Mike too needs to get time to think. In the managers' meeting, he might say to Jack—or, in fact, to all of them—"I've been blindsided by what's just been said. I would like to bring all this to a better outcome if I can. I need some time to pull my thoughts together. Then, when can we talk?"

If he can get the time, Mike would prep with the same Mock Interview strategy Jack used. But if Jack wants to get the whole thing over with right now, he may not be willing to set another time to talk. Mike would then need to feel his way along, still using the same Mock Interview points of strategy. Again, Mike doesn't want to wait until he's up to his neck in a difficult conversation to get the hang of balanced strategy. He wants to learn it, like CPR, before he needs it.

How would that work out for Mike? It would undoubtedly be excruciating. But these are good frameworks, and they give Mike more to do than take it on the chin or make it worse.

It's absolutely true that from everyone's perspective, the situation is complicated. But good strategy is not. Like others in these chapters, Jack and Mike would be able to follow this same pattern of strategy, even after a conversation had already begun to break down. Looking at our *preferred outcome*—where we would like to get in the conversation—will always be better than a blind reaction to whatever comes up. Framing our problem as a combination of our *preferred working relationship* and *interferences* doesn't just give us help from a standpoint of self-respect and respect for the problem; it makes us start there. The Mock Interview automatically builds in respect for our counterpart (see "Needed Now: Three-Way Respect").

A very tough conversation now has a real chance to find balance with respect. Will the conversation stop being difficult? No,

# Needed now: Three-way respect

The combat mentality, tough emotions, and doubts about both our counterpart's intentions and our ability to read them all make the choices we have in a difficult conversation appear simultaneously limited and extreme. Respect of any kind does not automatically come into play. But it's at times like this that we most need three-way respect as a strategy. If Jack wants to get this conversation right, he badly needs to put three-way respect into play now.

### Self-respect

It's easy to understand Jack's reluctance to confront Mike with his own disappointment in Mike's performance. Although Jack had power in the company and affection for Mike, the CEO needed more of Joan Didion's kind of self-respect—"doing things one does not particularly want to do." When he saw only two bad choices, Jack would have been hard put to figure out a self-respecting tack to take. If Jack changes what he's trying to do by starting with his preferred outcome, he won't think his options are limited to "don't confront" or "confront."

### Respect your counterpart

Up until the crisis in the senior managers' meeting, Jack behaved, paradoxically, as if he couldn't be friends with Mike *and* respect him—respect him in the sense of assuming that Mike could handle critical feedback and benefit from it. Then later, in the final confrontation, it would have seemed strange to Jack, if not impossible, to respect someone he had just voted down and who was now accusing him of betrayal. Wouldn't respect for Mike at that point have been weak or hypocritical? We make a mistake when we confuse respect with deference. Respect for your counterpart is no more deferential than self-respect is self-aggrandizing. Jack could avoid an adversarial view by taking the "two people who are not in accord now" view from chapter 4 and working from there.

### Respect the problem

In tough conversations, the topic is rarely the same as the problem. In Jack and Mike's case, the topic was their heretofore unproductive effort to turn the company around. The problem, however, was bigger than that; it was the whole bad deal: the poor results, yes, but also the tension in their friendship and the turmoil in the company. Bringing all this up front was exactly what Jack didn't want to do, so he avoided the conversation altogether. In fact, Jack avoided it until the problem itself confronted him in a crisis he couldn't control. But Jack didn't have to wait so long—instead he could plan strategy around where he wants to get in a tough conversation and what's in the way of getting there. He would be moving skillfully through the landscape of the conversation, instead of trying to skirt it.

### Three-way respect in play

Again using the Mock Interview, but now on the question of their first relationship—the one between two close friends working together—Jack could reaffirm his friendship for Mike and look straight at what's interfering with it: they have not clearly separated the side-by-side relationship between them as friends from the up-down relationship between them as CEO and senior vice president, and that has hurt them. In this new version, there's no trying to avoid a person, a problem, or a conversation. There is self-respect without self-aggrandizement. There is respect for the counterpart, with no hint of deference. And there is respect for the problem by placing it squarely in the landscape of the conversation without minimizing or exaggerating it.

because the situation isn't good, the atmosphere is oppressive, half the problems may be buried, and the stakes are high. But Jack and Mike are intentionally heading toward a better outcome. Like traceurs, they are looking at where they are and where they could move, and their reputations and relationships aren't taking such terrible hits.

## What to do: Tactics

If strategy gives Jack *what* he wants to say, tactics are *how* he will say it. We tend, mistakenly, to think that the trick to smoother conversations is a knack for tactics alone. We want to say the usual things that are hard for people to hear, but we want to say them without getting the bad reactions they usually get. That's asking tactics to do more than they can do. Trying to say bad things better so that we get a better response is much harder than having better things to say. That's why good tactics depend on good strategy.

At the same time, we do want to say the better things well, and in difficult conversations, that means collecting the tactics we've built up in this book.

### Don't guess: Assume innocent offensiveness

All too easily, people get caught up in a reaction loop in which difficult emotions seem to be an inescapable reaction to a counterpart's thwarting ploys. If Jack is angry and embarrassed because Mike's behavior toward the company's managers has been off-putting, it's a short step from there to the assumption that Mike personally is the trigger for Jack's own anger and embarrassment because Mike had offensive intentions in the first place. To close the loop, Jack retaliates as though Mike's bad intentions are at fault—that his intentions forced Jack into the embarrassing confrontation with Gus.

Jack can break out of that loop on his own, and assuming innocent offensiveness will help him there. By breaking the connection between the difficulty of the conversation and the assumption that it's his counterpart's fault, Jack is freed up to talk to Mike about the problem between them from a position of neutrality.

If, for example, Jack began with the assumption that Mike was creating a problem with the managers and offending them, but that Mike was *innocently* offending them, then very early on, Jack could have said to Mike, "This is working out in a way that you may not intend." By taking bad intentions on Mike's side out of his message, Jack doesn't have to worry about softening his message so that Mike can take it, or avoiding the conversation altogether because the problem of Mike's manner is too delicate a topic to raise at all.

It's possible, of course, that Mike is not innocently offensive. He could be offending the managers intentionally, whether because that's his strategy, or because it's a habit from his litigation days, or because he sees what he's doing in a different light and it looks legitimate to him. In any case, the working assumption that Mike is innocently offensive has no downside for Jack. It helps Jack open the topic, there's no negative effect on the friendship, and Jack can move wherever he wants from there.

### Take middle ground

Jack's new opening has put him on middle ground. He can move where he wants to go, or he can stay there no matter what comes at him from Mike. That's good, because however neutral Jack's opening is, Mike might escalate, resist, or push back against him.

Mike might push back if he himself is embarrassed and touchy because his efforts with managers have not been well received. So, in spite of Jack's neutral opening, Mike might snipe at him: "You can't make an omelet without breaking eggs, Jack. What did you expect?"

But Jack can stay on middle ground by granting Mike's premise and making his case from there: "You're right. Change isn't smooth. Some of the people here are trying hard, but they think you might be disparaging them more than revving them up. That's what I think you don't intend." A sniping remark from Mike might trigger Jack—no one likes a sarcastic comeback. But Jack has his attention on his own good tactic here, and he highlights what he *says* and lowlights how he *feels* in the moment. Tactics get him closer to a good outcome than reactions do.

### Immunize against thwarting ploys

It will be much easier for Jack to stay on middle ground if he knows which ploys lock onto his vulnerabilities. It's hard to take a mocking remark from a friend you're trying to help, but it has probably happened to Jack before. The question is whether Jack is vulnerable to the ploy, and if he is, what tactics will help him immunize. Granting Mike his premise and building his (Jack's) case from there is an example of the right kind of tactic, which is more valuable to Jack than trying to decide whether to take the punch or retaliate.

In fact, beginning to recognize the patterns in Jack and Mike's conversation is an immunization itself. We begin to step back and take a satellite view of what's happening in our own conversations. We can ask ourselves, "What did my counterpart just do, and what can I do when that happens?"

### Using the blueprint for speaking well in a tough moment

Specifically, how did Jack come up with the words for his new tactic? He used the blueprint: clear content, neutral tone, and temperate phrasing. Whether his habit in difficult conversations is to blurt or be silent, go soft or go blunt, attack or defend, or use any other loaded approach, he wants to trade it in for this one.

# Can Mike recover?

Of all the situations we have seen in this book, Mike's was the most dire. He faced the double whammy of a threat to his job and a threat to his most important friendship. Yet even in Mike's situation, the usual impediments in toxic conversations—combat mentality, emotional overload, misconceptions, and some impressive thwarting ploys—were in place, not new impediments. And as is usually the case, reputation and relationship were the most important qualities in jeopardy. Although the circumstances might change from conversation to conversation, the landscape of difficult conversations is basically the same, and the degree of strain will not change the fundamental characteristics of how to right what has gone wrong.

It would have been impressive if Mike had skillfully handled, right in the moment, the first conversation, when he was blindsided by Gus's and the other managers' attacks and by Jack's unsupportive response. It might have been even more impressive if Mike had handled the second conversation, alone with Jack, when Mike was vulnerable and Jack undermined and threatened him. But there is also skill in going back to repair the damage from a conversation that was handled unimpressively the first time. So while we could look at what Mike could have done differently in those first two conversations, we might do even better to look at what he could do now to recover, given where he ended up.

Considering the emotional reactions he (and Jack, too) has behind him, Mike would benefit from anything that would lighten the emotional load of the conversation. Putting self-respect and respect for his counterpart at the forefront would be a completely different starting point for Mike and a better place to put his mind to work. It is, specifically, the effort to find balance and respect that will open up new possibilities for him.

Because Mike and Jack had left off by attacking each other, professionally and personally, Mike will want to recover on both fronts going forward. He will have to act unilaterally, because there's no counting on Jack to help him now. To stay neutral, Mike will need to assume—as a working attitude—that Jack has been innocently offensive. And it will be especially important for Mike to change tack and find middle ground. But his range of response is, of course, as broad as anyone else's, and he can do it.

What would it look like if Mike recovered by using tactics we have seen before? If Mike's preferred outcome is to reestablish himself in the company, he might start with an opening that is focused, honest, and neutral. "I've already told Gus that what happened today caught my attention, Jack," he might begin. "I have been working up until now with fire in the belly, but less company knowledge than you or Gus or the other veteran managers have. I can see what this company can become, and I want to work with you and everyone else here toward that future with the same amount of enthusiasm I've had, and more skill. I don't want to leave this predicament where it is now."

If Mike wants to look at the problem from Jack's point of view, he might say, "The decision is yours, Jack, but right now the choices—who is going to quit or be fired—don't look good. I don't even think that's what Gus wants. We can try working together to open up some new possibilities to help you see your way clear."

If Mike wants to keep their friendship, he might say, "I don't want to continue working the way we have been, because I don't want to sacrifice twenty years of friendship by going down the wrong track. And if I can avoid it, I don't want you to see the friendship as contingent on the job, Jack. We've taken some hits today, but we're hockey players, so that's not the end of the world."

Where did Mike get the words for his tactics? He used the same blueprint Jack did in Jack's recast version: clear content, neutral tone, and temperate phrasing to say well what he wants and what he thinks.

Not much is changed here from other conversations in these chapters. Mike is taking a traceur's attitude, looking at where he is and which way he wants to move, where Jack is and where

Jack could move, where Mike wants to end up and what's in the way of getting there. He is looking for a balanced way forward, and three-way respect will see him through.

What's the outcome going to be for Mike and Jack? We don't know, because it won't be unilaterally determined by Mike. The future does not look completely cloudless even now. Mike doesn't know where Jack will take it from here, but Mike's recovery conversation won't make matters worse and may make them better.

## Reputation and relationships

What happens now between Jack and Mike, and how they handle themselves, will be read and interpreted by almost everyone else in the company. Unilaterally, Jack could rebalance this conversation—and so could Mike. If they do, they stand a good chance of protecting their reputations and relationships.

At this point, we might even step back and see a new loop emerging for difficult conversations. In practice, the tactics here take us out of the combat mentality, acknowledge our emotions while putting good tactics at the forefront, and do not depend on our being completely clear about our counterpart's intentions. All these tactics are built on respect: We respect our counterpart when we assume he is innocently offensive if his tactics are not well received. We respect ourselves when we talk to the ploys from middle ground, not passively and not aggressively. And we respect the problem in the landscape of the conversation when we stay with it skillfully, instead of avoiding it or reacting to whatever comes up.

Our new loop of three-way respect seems a long way from the failures to communicate that we started with in this book. But we shouldn't lose sight of where we've come from because too many of our counterparts, and too many tough conversations, are still caught in the old snarls of combat mentality, heavy emotional loads, and damaging misconceptions. For us, while those snarls are familiar, of course, they no longer predetermine that a conversation will blow up or break down. We have changed what *we* do. We have a clearer view of what happens in tough conversations— we can see them unfolding in recognizable and manageable ways. We have the skills to make our way through them in good balance, even when the conversations are unpredictable and big emotions are in play. And we have put three-way respect at the heart of our strategies because it is our best way out of failure-prone conversations with our reputations and relationships intact. The more of us there are who can right a conversation going wrong the better, so spread the word.

# NOTES

## Chapter 1

1. Names and identifying details have been changed.

## Chapter 2

1. Justice Potter Stewart, in obscenity case of *Jacobellis* v. *Ohio,* 378 U.S. 184 (1964). Stewart wrote that "hard-core pornography" was hard to define, but that "I know it when I see it." He later recanted this view in *Miller* v. *California,* 413 U.S. 15 (1973), in which he accepted that his prior view was simply untenable.

## Chapter 4

1. Joan Didion, "On Self-Respect," in *Slouching Towards Bethlehem* (New York: Farrar, Straus and Giroux, 1968), 142–148.

2. Andrea Estes, "Postgame Staffing Occupies Officials," *Boston Globe,* February 4, 2004.

3. Ken Auletta, "Beauty and the Beast," *New Yorker*, December 16, 2002, 64–81.

## Chapter 6

1. M. Lombardo and C. McCauley, *The Dynamics of Management Derailment*, technical report 34 (Greensboro, NC: Center for Creative Leadership, 1988).

## Chapter 7

1. The phrase "habit of mind" is from Joan Didion, *The Year of Magical Thinking* (New York: Knopf, 2005).

### Chapter 8

1. Ellen Barry, "Study Looks at Loss, Its Role in Depression: Finds Humiliation Triggers Worst Cases," *Boston Globe*, August 13, 2003, A3.

2. Melissa Bruder et al., *A Practical Handbook for the Actor* (New York: Vintage, 1986), 6–7, 72–73.

### Chapter 10

1. Linda Greenhouse, *Becoming Justice Blackmun* (New York: Times Books, 2005).

2. Ibid., 41

3. Ibid., 42.

4. Ibid., 45.

5. Ibid., 123.

# INDEX

## ACKNOWLEDGMENTS

My gratitude to John Lancaster for the happiness of our long friendship and writing liaison, knowing that I get more out of reading his writing than he gets out of reading mine. And my gratitude to Phyllis Strimling, Rob Scalea, and Neal Yanofsky, who have been unflaggingly loving and supportive. I could only get more out of our working relationship if we stopped laughing so much—and I wouldn't take the trade. To Diana and Peter Elvin, two nobles of kindness, who are warm and witty and wise. To Hollis Heimbouch, Jeff Kehoe, and the extended Harvard Business Press kinfolk for their many parts in this. My deepest appreciation to all the students and all the clients who were brave enough to take what we talked about, the "What do I do if?" and "What do I do now?" questions, then go again into some of the toughest conversations of their lives—and report back. And to J and R, who have listened more than any mortals should be asked to listen, my bottomless love.

## ABOUT THE AUTHOR

HOLLY WEEKS is the founder of Holly Weeks Communications, a communications consulting company, and a coach to executives and their organizations on negotiations, presentations, and writing, with a special emphasis on sensitive and difficult communications problems.

Holly has given her advice, strategies, and techniques for difficult communications in publications and broadcasts ranging from *Harvard Business Review* to *O, the Oprah Magazine* to ESPN Radio and CBS News Sunday. She is an advising expert on difficult communications for Harvard ManageMentor, a Conversation Starter on the HarvardBusiness.org blog, and a member of the Advisory Board of the Harvard Management Communication Letter.

At Harvard University, Holly is Adjunct Lecturer in Management Leadership and Decision Sciences at the Kennedy School of Government and Visiting Pro-Seminar Lecturer in Communication and the Vision Speech at the Graduate School of Education. She is also Senior Lecturer in Negotiation at the Simmons School of Management.

Holly was previously an Associate in Communications in the Harvard Business School MBA Program. As a Distinguished Instructor, she taught Management Communication and Negotiation and Conflict Resolution at the Radcliffe Institute of Harvard University. And she taught Expository Writing at Harvard College.

Holly received an AB *cum laude* in English and American Language and Literature from Harvard University and a Master's Diploma in Literature from the University of Edinburgh.

She lives in Cambridge, Massachusetts.